LAKE CHAMPLAIN
A
Natural History

Dedicated to Cedar

All rights reserved under International and Pan-American Copyright Conventions. No part of this book may be reproduced in any form or by any electronic, photographic, or mechanical means, including information storage and retrieval systems, without permission in writing from the publisher.

Library of Congress Cataloging-in-Publication Data

Winslow, Mike, 1968–

   Lake Champlain : a natural history / by Mike Winslow. — 1st ed.

     p. cm.

   Includes bibliographical references and index.

   ISBN 978-1-884592-51-5

   1. Natural history—Champlain, Lake. 2. Lake ecology—Champlain, Lake. 3. Champlain, Lake. I. Title.

   QH104.5.C35W56 2008

   508.743'1—dc22

                          2008037396

ISBN 978-1884592-51-5

©2008 The Lake Champlain Committee

First edition, First printing

Published by The Lake Champlain Committee

www.lakechamplaincommittee.org
106 Main Street Suite 200, Burlington, VT 05401-8434
Lori Fisher, Executive Director
Proceeds from this book will support the Lake Champlain Committee's work for a healthy, accessible lake.

   and

Images from the Past, Inc.

www.imagesfromthepast.com
PO Box 137, Bennington VT 05201
Tordis Ilg Isselhardt, Publisher

Printed in the USA

Design and Production: Toelke Associates, Chatham, NY

Printer: Versa Press, Inc., East Peoria, IL

Front cover photo: View from Mount Philo looking west, by Carolyn L. Bates

Back cover photos: Left, by Kevin Rose; center, by John Winton; right, by Trip Kinney

Opening illustrations for each chapter, along with details from these illustrations used throughout the book, © 2008 by Libby Davidson

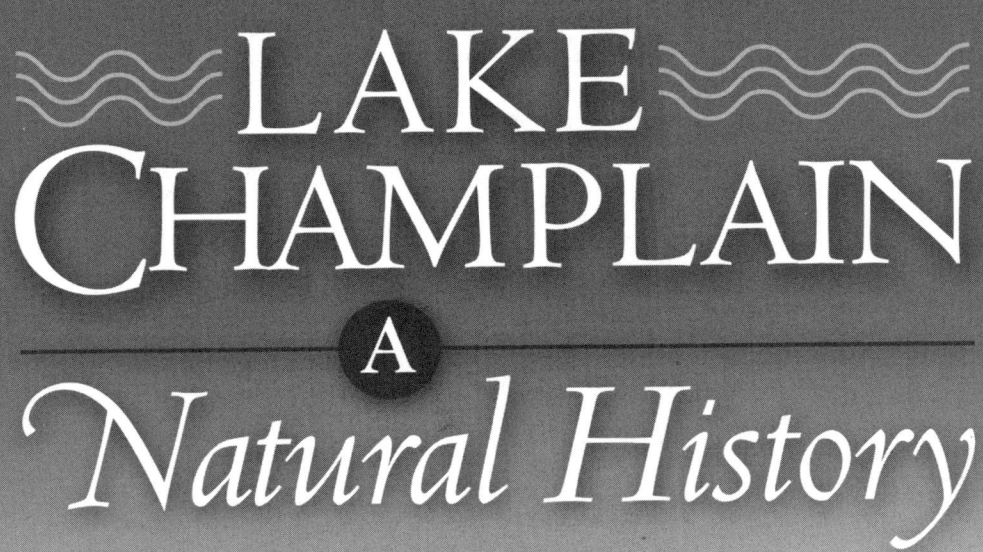

LAKE CHAMPLAIN
A Natural History

Mike Winslow

CONTENTS

FOREWORD — vi
PREFACE — viii
ABOUT THE LAKE CHAMPLAIN COMMITTEE — 1

1. THE SETTING — 3

The Origin of Lake Champlain — 4
The Sixth Great Lake — 10
In Lakes, Does Size Matter? — 12
Downhill Looking Up — 14
Five Lakes in One — 17
A Tale of Two Bays — 19

2. FORCES — 23

Retention Time — 24
Catching a Wave — 27
Autumn's Mix-up — 29
Slosh, Slosh — 31
Let There Be Light — 33
Lake Ice — 35
Understanding Your River — 39

3. PHENOMENA — 43

Thick Frothy Foam — 44
Streaking — 46
In a Fog — 48
Mirages — 50
Let It Snow — 52
The General — 55

4. LIVING LAKE: PLANTS   59

Where Land Meets Water   60
    Delta   60
    Beach   62
    Cedar Bluffs   64
Falling Leaves: Investing in the Food Chain   66
Putting Away the Groceries: Food Storage in Lake Champlain   69
Water Plants   71
Blue-green Algae: What's the Risk?   73
Little Glass Houses   76

5. LIVING LAKE: ANIMALS   79

A Night for the Birds   80
Dumpster Divers and Glorious Birds   82
Just Passing Through   85
Links in the Chain   88
Something Fishy   90
Fish Flu   94
Salmonid Challenges   96
    The Known: Sea Lamprey   96
    The New: Alewives   98
    The Mystery: Where Are the Young?   101
Holding an Eel by the Tail   103
Mishe-Nahma, King of Fishes   104
Degrees of Separation   107
Mini-Monsters, Little Wheels, Oar Feet, and Prongs   109
Home for the Holidays   112
Striding over the Water   114
Is a Mussel a Mussel?   116
A Long Winter's Nap   117

6. THE FUTURE OF LAKE CHAMPLAIN   121

Periodic Events and Predictability   122
Lag Times   123
Large-Scale Changes   125
    Land Use: Urban, Suburban   125
    Land Use: Agriculture   129
    Invasive Species   131
    Global Warming   134
The Value of the Lake   137

THE INDIVIDUAL'S ROLE   139
RESOURCES/BIBLIOGRAPHY   141
INDEX   148

FOREWORD

When the congressional kerfuffle erupted some years ago about whether Champlain was a Great Lake or not, I remember thinking: she's better than great. I've visited those other five; I've visited Lake Baikal too; all are wonderful. But the charm of Champlain lies in her unique scale, her constant mix of big and small.

There is no doubt, out on her waters, that you're on a substantial body of water—I've kayaked across keeping a very wary eye on the suddenly growing waves taking advantage of the long north-south fetch described so well in these pages, and I've seen the whiteout lake-effect snow that can blanket parts of Addison County early in the season. But on the lake you never feel truly remote from the opposite shore—the wonders are never lost to the curve of the horizon.

So: to sit on a dock in Panton on the Fourth of July and watch the fireworks go up over Port Henry. Or to circle the Four Brothers bird islands—but know that the barrooms of Burlington are but an hour or two's paddle away. Or to take the loveliest pause in any drive and cross the cable ferry at Ticonderoga, New York to Vermont, seven minutes shore to shore. Or to drive along the causeway to South Hero, or haunt the marshes at Missisquoi Bay. If you've got the legs, it's a two-day bike trip around the whole darned thing.

Sometimes, though, the lake feels so accessible that we almost take it for granted—I'm amazed, sometimes, by how few people are out there sailing on a lovely August afternoon (and how many of those that are have come from Canada!). Vermont is the Green Mountain State; the park across the water confines the Adirondacks: we tend to look up for definitions of our place, our identity. We're mountain people more than shoredwellers, perhaps.

But this book goes a long ways toward educating anyone who loves the sight of Lake Champlain. Beneath the glinting mirror you see from the road or the beach, there's a lovely and mysterious world. The mysteries have nothing to do with Champ—they're about how the lake's waters turn over in the course of a year, or why they are cold one day and warm the next, or who is living their life out unseen beneath the waves. Mike Winslow and Libby Davidson, with clear and lucid prose and accurate, charming illustration, answer dozens of questions that have occurred to me over the years, and better yet they answer questions it hadn't even struck me to ask. This is less like a field guide, and more like having a wise naturalist along with you on a trip.

Wise enough, it must be said, that they can't forgo discussing the very real challenges the lake faces. Mercury deposition, overfertilization, shoreline development, and of course the greatest challenge of all, global warming, all hang over Lake Champlain. We know from the long historical record that it is already behaving weirdly—failing to freeze far more often than the norm, for instance, with doubtless enormous short- and long-term effects on flora and fauna. But before you can save a place you have to love it, and before you can really love it you have to understand it. On the counts of both affection and insight this book is a tremendous success.

Bill McKibben

PREFACE

My undergraduate ecology professor once extolled the ecological significance of aspen trees, because their seeds fed so many creatures through the long winters. He inspired me to find out more about the species and what was known of its significance. I had a difficult time finding good references, however. Field guides provided little information about ecological attributes of species. Journal articles were so minutely focused and dense that I could glean little of consequence from them. What I needed was an introductory text written in compelling language.

I realized then, and have seen repeatedly since, that books about the natural world tend to come in two flavors. Either they are exasperatingly superficial or they are overwhelming complex, bogged down by mathematical formulas and jargon. As a writer, I have striven to find a voice between these extremes. *Lake Champlain: A Natural History* grew from a series of monthly columns written for the Lake Champlain Committee and distributed to members and newspapers throughout the Champlain Valley. The columns, begun in 2001, explore natural history and environmental issues facing the lake.

My overriding goal was to use the latest knowledge of lake ecology to examine interactions between biological, geological, and physical forces shaping the lake but in a style accessible to a lay audience. Some sections are based on a single article from scientific journals and how the research described there relates to the lake's ecology. Other sections draw from multiple sources and people, as well as my own lake explorations. The information is not original, but the format, presentation, and compilation are.

Lake Champlain offers an exemplary model of a large-lake ecosystem. Covering 425 square miles, it is the sixth-largest freshwater lake in the United States and shares many ecological characteristics with the Great Lakes, because of the similar climates. Yet Lake Champlain lacks human regulation of water levels and commercial navigational traffic, and as a result it hosts fewer nonnative species than the Great Lakes. Furthermore, the diversity of forms the lake takes, from the riverine South Lake to the broad, deep Main Lake, to shallow, 20,000-acre Missisquoi Bay, means the processes that occur there lend insights relevant to numerous other large bodies of water.

Sometimes referred to as the west coast of New England, Lake Champlain is a vital natural feature of the Northeast. The lake provides drinking water for approximately

200,000 people. Each year millions of seasonal visitors come to the lake to swim, fish, boat, and lounge upon the shores. They follow in the footsteps of those who first settled the region more than 10,000 years ago and who made the lake a wilderness highway. Subsequently the lake became the principal trading route between New York City and Montreal and as such played a pivotal role in the French and Indian and Revolutionary wars and the War of 1812.

The principal purpose of *Lake Champlain: A Natural History* is to share with readers my fascination with the lake, to deepen the sense of place that Lake Champlain inspires in so many people—but there is also a secondary purpose. Too often, public debates about lake management are guided by assumptions that are invalid. For example, it is often assumed that sea lamprey recently decimated trout and salmon populations—yet there were no such populations to decimate, since they had been extirpated from the lake over a century ago (although lamprey have complicated efforts to restore these populations). There is also an assumption that human-caused pollution has plagued the lake with algae blooms; but such blooms are mostly limited to shallow northern bays, and for reasons having at least as much to do with geology and topography as human influence. In fact, improvements in wastewater treatment facilities and the banning of phosphorus from laundry detergents greatly reduced the amount of nutrient pollution entering the lake; but these changes largely occurred before the systematic long-term monitoring of lake health began, so effects are quite difficult to evaluate. I hope that by discussing some of the background of lake management issues, *Lake Champlain: A Natural History* will help better inform the debate about the lake's future and stimulate stewardship efforts among the people that live and play in the region.

○ ACKNOWLEDGMENTS

Foremost among those deserving thanks are the staff and board of the Lake Champlain Committee, who gave me the freedom and opportunity to write. In particular, Lori Fisher has provided much of the drive behind the project. Her belief in the value of a book about Lake Champlain's natural history never wavered. A board committee of Sharon Murray, Tim Mihuc, Jim Schweithelm, and Mary Van Vleck kept the project on track and provided critical review of an early draft. Jeanne Stark helped coordinate everything in the office while I worked on the book, and Allison Freeman ably tracked down photographs and provided assistance and input as needed.

Much of the material in this book first appeared in a series of newspaper columns. The publications that carried that original work deserve praise for providing me a reason to keep writing. In particular, the *Plattsburgh Press Republican*, the *Colchester Sun*, *The Islander*, and the *North Avenue News* have been longtime, consistent supporters.

Many people assisted with technical review. Doug Facey and Ellen Marsden offered input on the Living Lake section, while Paul Marangelo provided insight on mussels. Tom Manley helped me understand the various currents and flows in the lake. Pat Manley, Mary Watzin, and Tom Manley introduced me to the pockmarks beneath Lake Champlain. Charlotte Mehrtens sat down with me to discuss Lake Champlain geology, and Peter Ryan provided review of the geology pieces. Bill Howland gave very careful, detailed review of the entire Forces and Setting sections. I also thank all the researchers listed in the resources section; without their work I would have nothing to write about. Any errors that remain are of course my own.

Working with editor Glenn Novak has been a real pleasure, and I truly appreciate his eye for detail. Tordis Isselhardt helped pull together our production team and keep us on task with unfailing good humor and energy. Book designer Ron Toelke and illustrator Libby Davidson collaborated to craft a beautiful product. Carolyn Bates, Gwen Dunnington, Shawn Good of the Vermont Fish & Wildlife Department, Ron Haskell, Trip Kinney, Megan Epler Wood, Kevin Rose, Mark Snelling, Jeanne Stark, and John Winton generously shared photos from their lake outings. Carolyn Bates has been especially accommodating, taking photos upon request and sometimes dropping everything to head into the field when conditions were right. Jeff McMahon, Bob McKearin, Marty Feldman, and Light-Works also provided assistance.

Thanks to Bill McKibben for his foreword. Jeff Hughes helped me develop an approach to writing about the natural world. Mark Lapin unknowingly gave me the framework for the book. Mary Watzin has repeatedly shared her tremendous knowledge of the lake. Finally, I extend huge thanks to Kira and Cedar; may our adventures on and around the lake continue.

ABOUT THE LAKE CHAMPLAIN COMMITTEE

The Lake Champlain Committee (LCC) was formed by New York and Vermont citizens in 1963 to prevent the lake from becoming an international commercial seaway for oceangoing vessels. Since then, the bi-state environmental organization has played a role in every major lake issue, from preventing a nuclear power plant on the Charlotte shore to developing an international water-quality agreement to reduce nutrient pollution. Throughout its history LCC has based its positions on sound science, provided a whole-lake perspective on issues, and helped craft solutions to water-quality problems. LCC is dedicated to protecting Lake Champlain's environmental integrity and recreational resources and fostering lake stewardship. The organization launched the longest-running citizen monitoring program in the country, developed the Lake Champlain Paddlers' Trail, and has a many-decade track record of educating and engaging citizens in lake protection. Publishing *Lake Champlain: A Natural History* is a continuation of the organization's long-standing efforts to increase people's understanding of the lake and involve them in its care. To learn more about LCC's work or to become a member, go to www.lakechamplaincommittee.org or call (802) 658-1414.

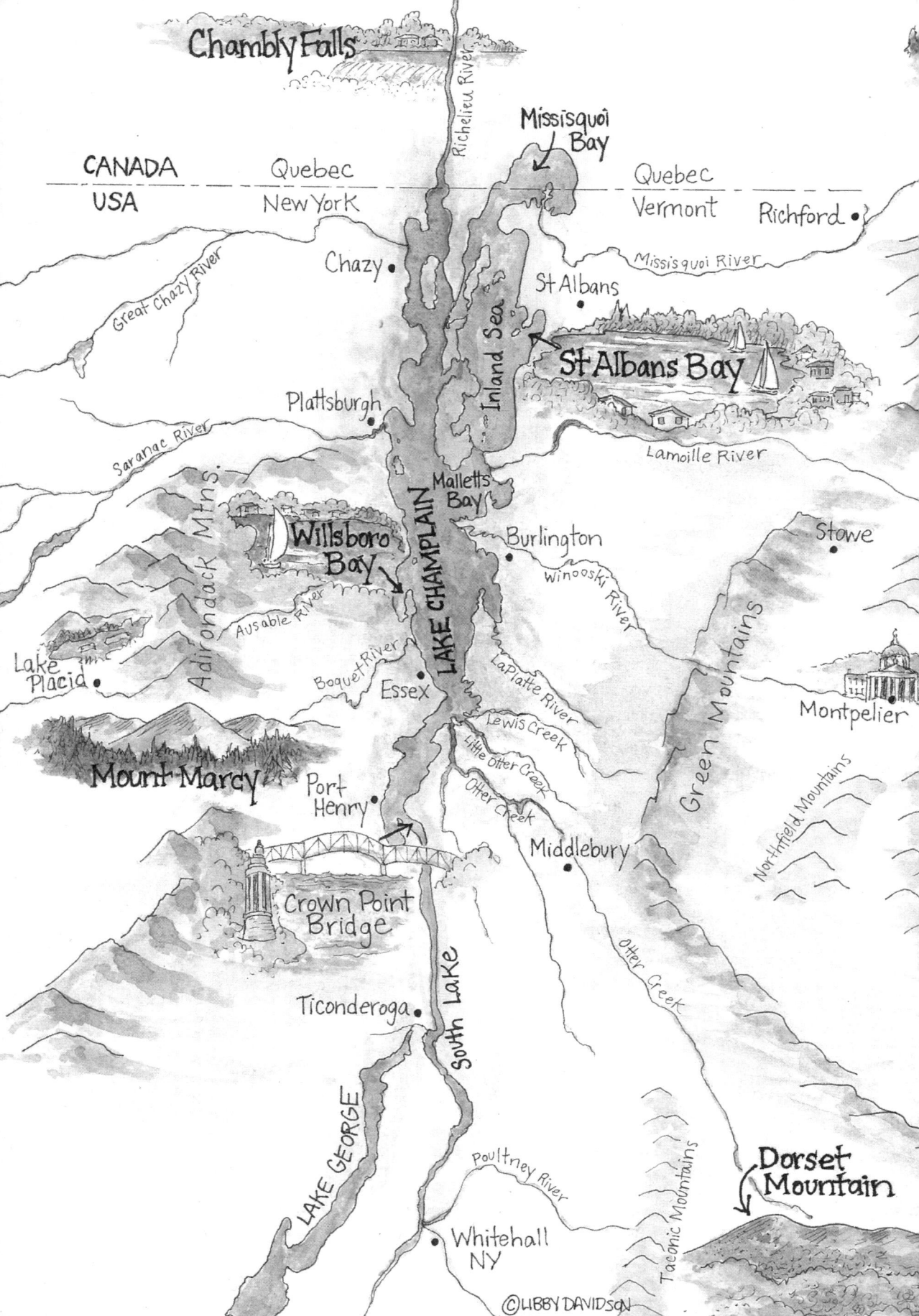

THE SETTING

Wind ruffles your hair, and the rumble of powerful engines fills your ears when you stand on the ferry deck for the trip between Charlotte, Vermont, and Essex, New York. The ride takes only twenty minutes but provides a stunning introduction to Lake Champlain. The Adirondack Mountains loom to the west, while the Green Mountains stand off to the east. The Four Brothers Islands sit shimmering on the northern horizon, while Thompson's Point and Split Rock Point pinch the lake to the south. Nearly 400 feet below lies the lake bed. Some residents and visitors may be content with this picture of the lake—its scenery and dimensions. However, the truly curious will want to know much more. The unique essence of Lake Champlain—its physical, chemical, and biological character—is a product of its setting. It matters where the waters that fill the lake come from. It matters what landscape those waters flow through. It matters how the lake came to be where it is.

◯ The Origin of Lake Champlain

By the beginning of March, I usually get a sense that winter has gone on long enough. At least by then the days are getting longer; but the pristine, fresh white snows have turned to slush and mud and ice, and the season has lost its allure. Watching melt-filled gutters and raging streams on those first warm days of spring makes me wonder what the land would have looked like after more than 100,000 years of winter, the approximate life span of the last glaciers to blanket the Champlain Valley.

Without the Laurentide glaciers that covered northern North America, Lake Champlain would not exist. At its maximum extent, the glacial ice over the Champlain Valley was over a mile and a half thick; its weight compressed the land beneath it like a sponge. As the glacier thickened to the north, the ice flowed over the landscape, following the paths of least resistance through valleys, including the Champlain Valley. Along the way rocks and boulders that were dragged beneath the ice sheet acted like sandpaper rubbed against the land. Tracks of the ice sheet are still visible on the landscape in scratches on bedrock outcrops and patterns of deposited boulders transported far from their northern origin. The glacial scouring, coupled with an influx of fresh water when the ice melted, has bequeathed us the lake we now enjoy.

Lake Champlain was not the first water body to occupy the postglacial Champlain Valley. About 18,000 years ago the glaciers reached their southernmost extent, depositing debris on present-day Long Island and Cape Cod, and then began to retreat. Mountains previously covered by ice became visible. Massive chunks of ice, left in depressions about the landscape, would melt and become kettle ponds. For a long period the remaining glacier prevented any northward flow of water, forcing drainage south to the Atlantic via the Hudson River. This was the era of Lake Vermont. The lake's waters lapped against the foothills of the Green Mountains, turning prominent peaks like Mount Philo in Charlotte, Vermont, into islands, and covering the sites of present-day Plattsburgh, New York, and Burlington, Middlebury, and even Montpelier, Vermont. At first, the southern terminus of this lake probably sat near Albany, New York, but later drainage occurred near Fort Ann, New York, 500 feet higher than the present water level. A forty-story building on today's lakeshore would have been underwater.

THE SETTING

Geologist Steven Wright describes the scene thousands of years ago:

> Lake Vermont was not a clean lake, but instead contained muddy water. Some of the mud washed off the recently deglaciated and poorly vegetated mountains bordering the lake, but a lot of mud was also pumped into the lake from streams flowing off the melting glacier, especially those streams flowing in tunnels within the ice, near its base. These high-pressure streams were like fire hoses at the front of the glacier spewing cold, dirty water into the lake.

One of the more dramatic events to shape the Champlain Valley occurred at the end of this ice age. To the west of Lake Vermont stood glacial Lake Iroquois, the precursor to Lake Ontario, approximately 300 feet higher in elevation and separated from Lake Vermont by a wall of ice. Eventually that wall gave way and water roared eastward from Lake Iroquois into Lake Vermont, across what is now northern Clinton County, New York, stripping away soil and carving deep gouges in the sandstone. Now, 12,000 years later, these areas, referred to as flat rocks or pavement barrens, still have little to no soil, and the mighty rivers that formed the gouges are only rivulets.

By about 12,000 years ago, the glacier had retreated far enough north to allow water to escape via the St. Lawrence estuary. According to Wright:

> Lake Vermont ended catastrophically when the glacial ice dam that was preventing its water from flowing north failed.... The failure of the dam allowed a huge volume of fresh water (hundreds of cubic kilometers) to roar out into the Atlantic Ocean through the Gulf of St. Lawrence. In the Burlington area the water level fell almost 100 m [more than 300 feet] within a matter of hours or days at most, exposing huge areas that were formerly under the muddy water of Lake Vermont.

However, the land had been depressed so much that it was actually below sea level, and the ocean soon advanced. For the next 2,000 years the brackish water of the Champlain Sea covered the valley. This water body was intermediate in depth between Lake Vermont and present-day Lake Champlain. A forty-story building on today's lakeshore would have stuck above the surface, but a twenty-five-story building would not. The salt water brought with it a distinctive biota, including whales and seals—now left only in bones—and sea lamprey and rainbow smelt, which have since adapted to a freshwater existence.

At its greatest extent, the Champlain Sea covered the areas around Montreal and the Ottawa River valley, in addition to the Champlain Valley. Over time, the earth that had been depressed by the glaciers rebounded, and the sea shrank. Cut off from the Atlantic, the salt sea eventually became diluted, until it was fresh. The area covered by the Champlain Sea shrank to the size of the Lake Champlain we know today.

Though the glaciers that covered the Champlain Valley carved out Lake Champlain, their actions were superimposed on a landscape already prepared to host a lake. Movements of the earth's crust millions of years earlier had set the stage. According to plate tectonic theory, thick slabs of the earth's outermost crustal layer of continents and ocean floors float over a denser, viscous rock layer, moving about through the eons. Sometimes the slabs bump into each other, and mountains form

Lake Champlain was not the first water body to occupy the postglacial Champlain Valley. (photo by Gwen Dunnington)

as the converging slabs crumple. In other places the plates pull apart and ocean basins develop between them. While all this pulling and pushing creates massive features like mountains and oceans, it also has smaller-scale, more localized, effects. The stories of the mountains around Lake Champlain have been well told by others, but the geologic conditions that led to the lake itself have received less attention.

Two factors made what is now the Champlain Valley better suited to host a large lake than any of the surrounding area between Lake Ontario and the Connecticut River. First, a valley probably already existed here. Second, the bedrock was softer and easier to erode than in the surrounding mountains.

The story of the preexisting valley began perhaps 160 million years ago. At that time, all the continental plates were knit together in the supercontinent known as Pangaea, with what was to become the Champlain Valley located near the center. The Green Mountains already towered over the area. The Adirondacks we know had not yet arisen, though the rock that would become the Adirondacks was in place, and other mountains had previously existed there.

But Pangaea was beginning to break apart. What would become the continental plates of North America, Africa, and Eurasia began to separate; new oceanic crust formed between them; and the Atlantic Ocean grew. As the plates pulled apart, the continental crust stretched like pizza dough. In some places, lava squirted up through rips in the crust, forming volcanoes. In other areas rock layers cracked and shifted, forming faults and folds. Many of these faults lay along what is now a north-south orientation, parallel to the movement of the crusts.

Between two of these parallel faults, large blocks shifted downward, forming a graben (German for ditch). Imagine holding a deck of cards perpendicular between your hands. By squeezing the cards you can keep the deck whole; but if you briefly relax your grip, the center portion slips downward. The breaks between the cards represent faults. The cards that fall are the graben.

Like many of the world's most impressive water bodies, Lake Champlain occupies a graben. Russia's Lake Baikal, the world's deepest lake, formed in a graben, as did Lake Tahoe. Both the Dead Sea and the Red Sea in the Middle East owe their existence to grabens. Graben formations may be as large as the East African Rift Valley or as small as a reach of the Boquet River.

Evidence of a massive downfall of rocks can be seen up and down the eastern seaboard, with Lake Champlain at the northern end. As a whole the formation is called the Great Valley. "In Maryland the Great Valley is the Hagerstown Valley; in Pennsylvania it is the Cumberland, Lebanon and Lehigh Valley respectively from south to north. The Great Valley cuts across northern New Jersey and up into New York as the Hudson Lowlands," says geologist Jane Ansley.

The effects of the graben-forming fault can be seen at the Palisades, the cliffs located in the Split Rock area between Essex and Westport, New York, on the shore opposite the mouth of Otter Creek. Here, the older metamorphic rocks on the west side tower 800 to 1,000 feet over the lake. The lake itself reaches more than 300 feet in depth here. Meanwhile, on the Vermont shore, less than two miles from the cliffs, the bedrock is composed of softer limestones. The valley limestones probably dropped many thousands of feet relative to the adjacent rocks of the New York side.

Even millions of years before the glaciers arrived, the graben had likely widened and deepened. The surrounding mountains would have prevented water from escaping in other directions. The ancient rivers that drained these mountains left few traces; most water bodies are ephemeral in geologic terms. However, water flowing off them would have sought planes of weakness in the rocks of the graben, eroding the ditch over time.

Such erosion would have been facilitated by the second factor in our tale, the relative softness of the underlying bedrock. The bedrock of the Champlain Valley is predominately limestone and dolomite, both calcium carbonate–based rocks. Calcium carbonate dissolves in weak acids, and rainwater is naturally acidic because of the presence of carbon dioxide in the atmosphere. Over time these factors can work to weaken rock tremendously. For example, many of the world's most impressive natural cave formations, like Mammoth Cave in Kentucky, occur in limestone. Meanwhile the bedrock of the surrounding mountain is quartzite and granite, rocks much harder and more resistant.

The valley bedrock formed long before the graben dropped down, long before Pangaea had formed, somewhere between 560 million and 455 million years ago. At that time what is now the eastern United States was covered by a warm, shallow ocean. Warm because the area was located closer to the equator. Shallow because the ocean water sat over the edge of the thick continental crust—as the Mediterranean Sea or the Bahama shelf does today—rather than the thinner crust that lies beneath the oceans. Meanwhile, corals and other sea creatures with shells of calcium carbonate inhabited this ocean. Over millions of years these shells fell to the sea floor when the organisms died, mixed with sediments washing in from the surrounding land, and with time and pressure formed today's limestone and dolomite. Meanwhile, the entire region drifted northward upon shifting tectonic plates to its present location. Remnants of these early coral reefs with fossils intact can still be found throughout the Champlain Valley, with some of the best examples preserved on Grand Isle and Isle La Motte in the middle of Lake Champlain, and at Crown Point, New York.

So when the glaciers arrived, the stage had already been set. The graben had produced a valley through which they could flow. Soft sedimentary rocks composed the bedrock of that valley. Years of rainwater and running water had weakened the bedrock. As the ice sheets oozed through, pushing their layer of rocks beneath them like sandpaper, it was easy enough to deepen the Champlain Valley before filling it with meltwater when the ice finally retreated.

Though Lake Champlain seems such an integral part of our landscape, it too has changed and will continue to change. Many low areas, once underwater, have since been mantled with sediment eroded from the surrounding mountains; areas that are now lowlands of the Champlain Valley have slowly transitioned from water to wetland to dry land. The process continues today, exemplified by the river deltas forming at the mouth of the lake's largest rivers or in the southern part of the lake where lazy sloughs fill with vegetation. Older deltas from the Winooski River can be found as far inland as Hinesburg, Vermont. A continuing challenge for lake lovers is distinguishing manageable changes from inevitable ones.

The bedrock of the Champlain Valley is predominantly limestone and dolomite. (photo by Trip Kinney)

○ The Sixth Great Lake

For a brief period in 1998, the U.S. government officially recognized Lake Champlain as one of the Great Lakes. The designation allowed Vermont institutions access to funds reserved for states that bordered an ocean or one of the Great Lakes, but Midwestern officials were outraged that Champlain might share this designation with their lakes. After much media attention and hyperbole, Congress rewrote the designation, and Lake Champlain reverted to an "almost" Great Lake, while retaining the funding opportunities.

Despite being the sixth-largest freshwater lake in the United States, Champlain is still substantially smaller than any of the Great Lakes. By surface area, almost seventeen Champlains would fit into Ontario, the smallest of the Great Lakes. By water volume, almost nineteen Champlains would fit into Lake Erie, which contains less water than Ontario. Only in depth does Champlain come close to any of the Great Lakes, topping shallow Lake Erie in both maximum and average depth.

Aside from the legal ramifications of a Great Lake designation for Champlain, there are geographical and ecological considerations

Looking west to Juniper Island (photo by Carolyn L. Bates)

that link the water bodies. By virtue of sitting on similar latitudes, the Great Lakes and Champlain share similar catchment ecosystems, dominated by deciduous forests and seasonal climates. The systems have similar glacial histories and even share a hydrologic connection through the New York State Canal System and the St. Lawrence River, which has allowed many of the exotic species that arrive in the Great Lakes on commercial ships eventually to reach Champlain.

After the glaciers retreated, the hydrologic connection was even more pronounced. For a period the Great Lakes and Champlain (at the time Lake Vermont) all drained to the Atlantic via the Hudson River. Later the Great Lakes' drainage shifted to the north via the St. Lawrence River while ice still blocked the St. Lawrence's passage to the ocean, so the Great Lakes drained through Lake Vermont.

Today, both systems drain to the St. Lawrence River, so it would seem they could be considered part of the same drainage basin. Yet when the Great Lakes Commission, a binational entity charged with overseeing lake management, outlined its position regarding adding Lake Champlain to the Great Lakes, one of its principal lines of reasoning noted that Champlain was "outside the Great Lakes Basin." So which is it? Do Lake Champlain and the Great Lakes share a drainage basin?

The simple definition of a drainage basin, or catchment, is that part of the land occupied by a drainage *system*—namely, a stream or a body of impounded surface water together with all tributary streams and bodies of impounded surface water. By this definition, all land is located within some basin. The size of a drainage basin depends on which drainage point is being referred to. The term *watershed* is often used interchangeably with drainage basin, but it more specifically refers to the dividing line between two drainage basins.

Drainage basins, or catchments, are like Russian matryoshka dolls, small ones nestled inside larger ones. When defining a basin, like the Lake Champlain basin or the Great Lakes basin, one defines the largest doll. Within the Lake Champlain basin lie the smaller dolls of the Saranac River basin, the Winooski River basin, the Au Sable River basin, and many others. Each of these in turn could be separated into yet smaller basins. However, the St. Lawrence River basin would be a larger doll that encompasses both the Great Lakes and Champlain basins. The Atlantic Ocean drainage basin would be larger still.

People are usually most concerned about water bodies with which they are most familiar, the places where they swim, fish, or boat. A resident of Lake Placid would probably express more interest in the Lake Placid basin than the Lake Champlain basin, even though one is nestled within the other. And residents of the Midwest are more concerned about a Great Lakes basin than the larger St. Lawrence River basin. Truth be told, advocates for Lake Champlain are more likely to be concerned about the Lake Champlain basin than the larger St. Lawrence River basin, too.

However, a narrow focus can make managing larger drainage basins difficult. Problems in the receiving water body may seem remote to people in smaller areas that appear clean. In October 2005 Vermont ordered work stopped on a golf course at Jay Peak because the developer had failed to control erosion at the site; the resort later paid $105,000 for violating stormwater runoff rules. The site drains to Missisquoi Bay, the most degraded section of Lake Champlain, yet distant enough from the mountain that water quality protection there did not receive appropriate attention. An extreme example occurs in the Gulf of Mexico, where a large excess of nutrient pollution has created a "dead zone," yet the source of most nutrients is far upstream, in the heart of the Midwest along the Mississippi River and its tributaries.

On the plus side, however, when an emotional attachment to a local water body energizes more people, the focus on smaller drainage basins has positive downstream effects. Numerous tree plantings and volunteer activities such as river cleanups have been conducted throughout the Lake Champlain basin by people who wanted to help their nearby river—but also perhaps the lake into which that river flows. Similarly, allowing institutions in the Lake Champlain basin to make use of resources previously reserved for the Great Lakes has increased the breadth and diversity of ideas and research brought to bear on Great Lakes issues. And these ideas can be transferred farther downstream to improve the St. Lawrence River, too. Water links communities across surprisingly broad geographic spans.

◯ In Lakes, Does Size Matter?

If you were asked to identify the largest student in the local high school, would you pick the seven-foot basketball player or the shorter 275-pound offensive lineman from the football team? Both have legitimate claims to the title "largest," depending on how size is measured. Similarly, there are different ways to measure size in lakes.

Lake Champlain is often cited as the sixth-largest freshwater lake in the United States, a distinction based on the 435-square-mile surface area of the lake. Only the five Great Lakes are larger in surface area. (But there is that caveat about fresh water: Great Salt Lake in Utah has more than four times the surface area of Lake Champlain.)

When it comes to volume of water in a lake, the runner-up to the Great Lakes is Lake Tahoe on the California-Nevada border. Tahoe holds fourteen times more water than Lake Champlain, despite having less than half the surface area. Lake Tahoe is phenomenally deep. At its maximum, Tahoe is over 1,600 feet deep, compared to just over 400 feet for Lake Champlain and 1,330 feet for Lake Superior, the deepest of the Great Lakes.

But Lake Tahoe isn't even the deepest lake in the United States. That distinction belongs to Crater Lake in Oregon—over 1,900 feet deep. Both Crater Lake and Lake

THE SETTING

Tahoe formed when geologic events exposed deep openings inside the earth. Crater Lake formed when water from ice and snow filled the collapsed funnel of a massive volcano. Lake Tahoe formed along geologic fault lines, a process that has produced most of the world's deepest lakes, including Lake Baikal, which is 5,712 feet deep.

Each of these measures of size—surface area, volume, and depth—has different ecological consequences. Of course the three measures are not unrelated to one another, so there is overlap in how they affect lake functions.

Surface area is probably the best measure of a lake's influence on the surrounding landscape. The larger the area of a lake, the more energy it can absorb from the sun in a given season. Since water heats and cools more slowly than land, lakes with large surface areas moderate the weather of the surrounding basin. Spring temperatures are somewhat cooler as the lake absorbs much of the early season heat energy; autumn temperatures are warmer as the lake slowly relinquishes heat absorbed through the summer. Also, the larger the surface area of the lake, the greater the distance winds can blow without interruption, increasing the ability of the lake to affect shoreline climates.

The total amount of energy a body of water can absorb is determined by its volume. It takes one (nutritional) Calorie of heat to raise the temperature of one kilogram of

Leddy Beach, Burlington (photo by Carolyn L. Bates)

water one degree Celsius. In other words, if a hamburger has 400 Calories, it would take the energy of 65 million hamburgers to raise Lake Champlain's temperature one degree, and 937 million hamburgers to raise Lake Tahoe's temperature one degree.

Depth influences the internal mixing processes of a lake. Most lakes naturally stratify during the summer, with warm water over cooler water. In the spring and autumn these layers then mix. Very deep lakes never mix, because they can't absorb enough energy to heat the deepest coldest water. Very shallow lakes are always mixing, because heat energy penetrates to the bottom of the lake, and wind stirs them from top to bottom.

The depth of a lake also influences development of flora. Rooted plants can develop in all areas of a lake where light penetrates to the bottom. Some very shallow water bodies, like Lake Chad in Africa (nearly 10,000 square miles of surface area but an average depth of only five feet), are more akin to wetlands than lakes. In Lake Champlain, extensive shallow areas are found in the southern end of the lake and Missisquoi Bay.

There is one measure by which Lake Champlain exceeds other large lakes in North America—the ratio of the drainage basin to lake surface area. Every acre of Lake Champlain receives drainage from 17.6 acres of land. An acre of water in the Great Lakes drains only between 1.5 acres of land for Lake Superior and 4.0 acres for Lake Ontario.

Because of the high ratio of basin area to lake area, the surrounding landscape has a greater effect on Lake Champlain than it does in the Great Lakes. If each acre of basin is seen as a potential source of sediment or pollution, and thus capable of putting one figurative nick in the lake, then more acres are more small cuts that can add up to gaping wounds for Lake Champlain. The high ratio is particularly pronounced in the smaller lake segments of Missisquoi Bay (36:1) and the southern part of the lake (55:1), where the problem is compounded by the relatively small water volume of these shallow segments. While catchment area to lake surface area ratio explains many of the differences in water quality between lake segments, there are other important factors, as we shall see later.

○ Downhill Looking Up

A bedrock sill overlain by glacial deposits forms the head of a series of rapids in the Richelieu River at St-Jean-sur-Richelieu, Quebec. In the twelve miles between St-Jean and Chambly, downstream to the north, the river falls approximately eighty feet. In 1609 Samuel de Champlain described the scene from the Chambly side:

> The approach to the rapids is a sort of lake into which the water flows down, and it is about three leagues in circumference. Nearby are meadows where no Indians live, by reason of the wars. At the rapids there is very little water, but it flows with great swiftness, and there are many rocks and boulders, so that

the Indians cannot go up by water; but on the way back they run them very nicely. All this region is very level and full of forests, vines and butternut trees. No Christian has ever visited this land and we had all the misery of the world trying to paddle the river upstream.

Waters flow downhill, pulled by gravity, and St-Jean is Lake Champlain's "downhill." All water that flows out of the lake passes through these rapids. A droplet of rainwater may land in the High Peaks of the Adirondacks, or on a small pond near Vermont's Northeast Kingdom, or on the Taconic Mountains of southern Vermont, or in Quebec's Eastern Townships, but it crosses the Lake Champlain watershed here. Mount Marcy is the highest peak in New York State and stands seventy-five miles southwest of St-Jean, over 5,000 feet above the surface of the lake. Coits Pond lies in Cabot, Vermont, about a mile shy of the county border that defines the Northeast Kingdom, and at the headwaters of the Winooski River sixty-five miles southeast of St-Jean. Dorset Mountain of the Taconics straddles the border of Rutland and Bennington counties in Vermont 125 miles to the south. Lac d'Argent can be found in Eastman, Quebec, at the headwaters of the Missisquoi River fifty miles northeast. All four of these places lie within the Lake Champlain catchment. From each, our water droplets follow gravity's pull through the drainage basin to the lake:

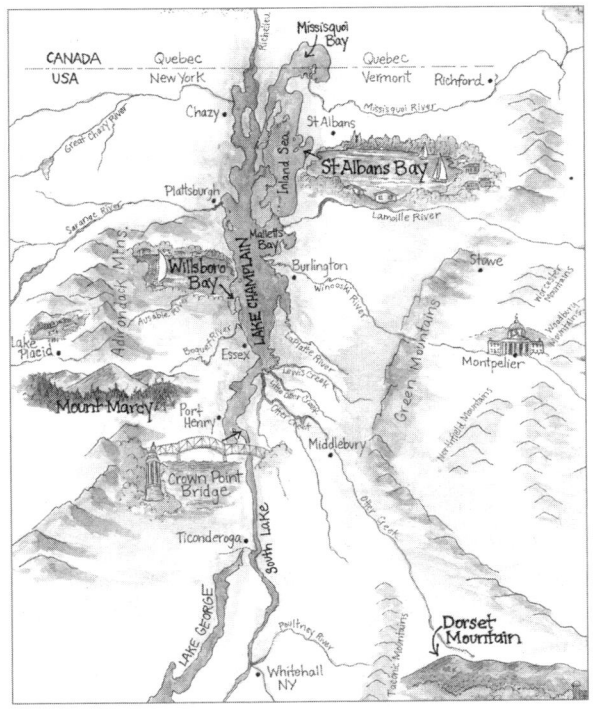

The Mount Marcy droplet passes through the High Peaks of the Adirondacks on an incredibly scenic voyage, cascading off the east side of the mountain and tumbling into Ausble Lakes, then traveling northeast in the Ausable River. Before reaching Lake Champlain near Port Kent, New York, the droplet falls over ninety feet in elevation for each of the thirty-five miles it traverses and passes through two miles of spectacularly carved and sculpted rocks in the Ausable Chasm.

The Coits Pond droplet enters directly into the Winooski River and flows south for three miles before turning west. It then flows eighty-eight miles through towns and villages, past the Vermont state capital, along Interstate 89, and then through the more urbanized Chittenden County before entering the lake at Colchester, Vermont.

From Dorset Mountain the droplet's trip differs depending on whether it falls off the southwest side of the mountain or the northeast side. If it falls on the southwest, it goes into the Mettawee River and flows forty-one miles northwest through both New York and Vermont to the Champlain Canal just upstream of the southern tip of the lake in Whitehall, New York. Along the way north it passes through the narrow South Lake and past historic Fort Ticonderoga, before gliding under the Crown Point Bridge. If the droplet falls on the northeast side, it enters the Otter Creek, the longest river in the basin, and flows north for over a hundred miles, passing through swamps and farmland, over waterfalls, and through long, lazy reaches, before arriving at the lake just south of its midpoint.

The droplet from Lac d'Argent journeys almost as far, about ninety-five miles, before coming into the lake. It first heads south, but just before the international border it joins the main stem of the Missisquoi River and turns west. Eventually the droplet enters the United States at Richford, Vermont, and follows Routes 105 and then 78 to Missisquoi Bay.

Cave in ledge near Burlington (photo by Carolyn L. Bates)

Once in the lake most of the water follows a much slower route toward St-Jean. Our transformed droplets flow leisurely northward through the Main Lake and skirt the western side of Grand Isle County, Vermont. There is little difference in elevation between where the water enters the lake and the rapids at St-Jean: about one foot over the more than twenty miles between Rouses Point and St-Jean, and a little over a foot in the thirty miles between Whitehall and the Main Lake. The Whitehall trip is the longest, at 120 miles. The push of the wind and of water draining from tributaries affects the speed of transit more than does the drop in elevation at the falls.

The Missisquoi River droplet (the one from Lac d'Argent), however, follows a more tortuous path, first skirting the circumference of the bay. Though it entered the bay in the southeastern corner, discharged northward from the river's mouth, the only way for it to leave the bay is via the southwestern corner. And once it has left the bay, it may follow one of two paths. Both require southward flow, before a turn north. Most water from Missisquoi Bay takes the direct path through the Alburg Passage, between Alburg and North Hero; eventually this route reaches the Main Lake on the east side of Isle La Motte before turning north. The remainder of Missisquoi Bay's water enters the Inland Sea. Most of these droplets also pass through the islands, this time at the Gut, between North Hero Island and Grand Isle. However, some water continues southward through the Sandbar Causeway and enters Malletts Bay, finally reaching the Main Lake by passing through one of two portals in the railroad causeway at the west end of the bay. In the Inland Sea and Malletts Bay, narrow-flow pathways and multiple exit and entry points for water complicate the general gravitational currents.

Four droplets, at least four different paths, but one destination. Of course the trail is not nearly as simple as expressed here. Approximately half the water that lands in the drainage basin evaporates rather than runs off. Turbulence occurs at the mouths of rivers and at constrictions. The water is also pushed by wind and flows between areas of different densities. The internal movements of water can be even more important than the gravitational pull through the lake.

○ Five Lakes in One

The single entity of Lake Champlain contains five distinct segments, each with its own character: the South Lake, the Main Lake, and, east of the islands, Malletts Bay, the Inland Sea, and Missisquoi Bay.

The thin, narrow South Lake stretches thirty-miles between the lake's inlet at Whitehall, New York, and the Crown Point Bridge. This lake segment is much like a river in appearance, and earliest navigators actually referred to it as an extension of Wood Creek rather than Lake Champlain. The South Lake receives most of its water from three tributaries—the Poultney, Mettowee, and La Chute rivers. In all, more than 15 percent of the lake's drainage basin empties into this segment, which contains only 0.6 percent of the lake's water. Many invasive species, including water chestnut and zebra mussels, first appeared in the South Lake, having migrated via the Champlain Canal. The zebra mussels have increased the water clarity, allowing denser growth of water chestnut and other aquatic plants. The weeds provide great habitat for fish and wildlife but can make swimming and boating a challenge.

Between the Crown Point Bridge and Thompson's Point the lake transitions, showing characteristics of both the South Lake and Main Lake. Though not quite as narrow as the South Lake, this area at its greatest does not much exceed three miles in width; in depth it is more similar to the Main Lake, and Lake Champlain's deepest point, about 400 feet, lies just off Thompson's Point. North of Thompson's Point the lake widens considerably, presenting the broad scenic expanse that so many have come to treasure.

The Main Lake, stretching between Thompson's Point and the mouth of the Richelieu River, covers nearly 300 square miles and contains over 80 percent of the lake's water volume. The basin's two principal cities, Plattsburgh, New York, and Burlington, Vermont, sit on the shores of the Main Lake. As befitting its size, the Main Lake contains a diversity of habitats, including bright sand beaches, cobble shorelines, the stunning cliffs at the Palisades, and dots of islands poking above the water surface. The Green and Adirondack mountains, with their play of light and shadow, frame the vistas.

At about midpoint on the Main Lake's north-south axis, Grand Isle divides the waters. Areas west of Grand Isle are still considered part of the Main Lake. To the east sit Malletts Bay, the Inland Sea, and Missisquoi Bay.

Malletts Bay, the southernmost of these three eastern pieces, is isolated from other lake segments by an abandoned railroad causeway to the west and a road causeway to the north. Malletts Head and Red Rock Point pinch the bay into two distinct segments, an inner bay and an outer bay. The Lamoille River, the bay's largest tributary, enters the outer bay, while the Winooski River delta forms much of the southern boundary (though the Winooski itself drains to the Main Lake). The bay contains steep drop-offs to deep water; half the outer bay is over forty-nine feet deep, but at the same time nearly 40 percent of the bay is less than twenty feet deep. The greater water volume dilutes nutrients, and thus algae blooms are less frequent in Malletts Bay than in other lake segments. Malletts Bay hosts numerous marinas, since it is well sheltered from the weather, making it a very popular spot for boaters.

The Inland Sea, also referred to as the Northeast Arm, lies between Grand Isle and North Hero Island on the west and the shores of mainland Vermont on the east. It is not as broad or deep as the Main Lake but physically and chemically resembles a smaller version of it. The Inland Sea covers 104 square miles, with an average depth of forty-two feet.

Much of the Inland Sea is clear and cold, though shallow bays like St. Albans are more turbid. No major tributaries drain to this lake segment, a factor that likely helps protect its water quality. In recent years, however, a summer oxygen deficit in deeper portions of the water column has prompted concerns about a potential developing "dead zone."

Missisquoi Bay fills a shallow basin at the northeasternmost portion of the lake, only fourteen feet deep at its maximum, but with over thirty square miles of surface area. Though larger in surface area than Malletts Bay, Missisquoi Bay contains less than one-third the water volume because of its shallowness. Three significant tributaries discharge into Missisquoi Bay—the Pike River, the Rock River, and the Missisquoi River. The Pike and most of the Rock catchments lie within Quebec. The Missisquoi is the second-longest river draining to Lake Champlain and drains over 10 percent of the entire lake's catchment. High nutrient levels, which fuel algae growth, and extensive sedimentation from these rivers make Missisquoi Bay one of the murkier lake segments, but also enable the bay to host abundant wildlife and excellent warm-water fishing.

Like individual courses of a fine meal, the lake's segments blend together and add to the satisfaction of the whole. Each offers its own unique characteristics; together they magnify one another's charms.

○ A Tale of Two Bays

It was the best of times, it was the worst of times. So begins Charles Dickens's classic tale that weaves a story of eighteenth-century London and Paris. In that statement and the ensuing paragraphs, Dickens tries to capture the sense that all times are essentially the same, but those living in a particular time period feel compelled to describe their situation only in superlatives. Lake Champlain, too, is often described in superlatives, both positive and negative. It is "the jewel of New England," according to Senator Leahy of Vermont. Meanwhile, the Quebec environmental minister called the northwest portion of the lake an "ecological disaster." How can these two people be talking about the same water body?

Willsboro Bay on the New York shore and St. Albans Bay on the Vermont shore embody the contradictions and superlatives inherent in Lake Champlain. Both cover about 7.5 square miles and would seem at first glance to be very similar. Yet each year St. Albans Bay experiences algae blooms and reports of deplorable water quality, while Willsboro Bay remains clear and blue. Probing beyond a first glance reveals great differences in the two bays.

Three critical factors that make St. Albans Bay more susceptible to algae blooms are average wind direction, water depth, and the amount of nutrients in the water column.

In the summer, prevailing winds are from the south. Willsboro Bay opens to the Main Lake and the north, and so the prevailing winds promote water exchange. St. Albans Bay opens to the south, so prevailing winds inhibit water exchange. In addition, a south wind on St. Albans Bay will drive algae blooms onto shore, where they are even more noticeable.

Differences between the depths of the bays influence the summer water temperatures. Two bays with about the same surface area but differing in depth have vastly different quantities of water in them. The shallow bay, with much less water, heats and cools more quickly than the deep bay. Warm summer water temperatures invite algae blooms like a rotten cantaloupe calls fruit flies.

Willsboro Bay is deep, averaging fifty feet and plunging to nearly two hundred feet at its deepest. Although St. Albans Bay reaches a respectable maximum depth of sixty-four feet, the average is only eleven feet. That is shallow enough for sunlight to reach the bottom in many locations and to allow extensive growth of weed beds in addition to the algae.

Temperature and wind alone are not sufficient to explain the algae blooms, however; algae also need nutrition. The principal factors that influence the amount of nutrients available are the shape and size of the bays' basins and land uses in those basins.

Water bodies collect nutrients from the surrounding land. In flat areas there is more land to contribute nutrients than in steep areas. Therefore, one finds more nutrient-rich

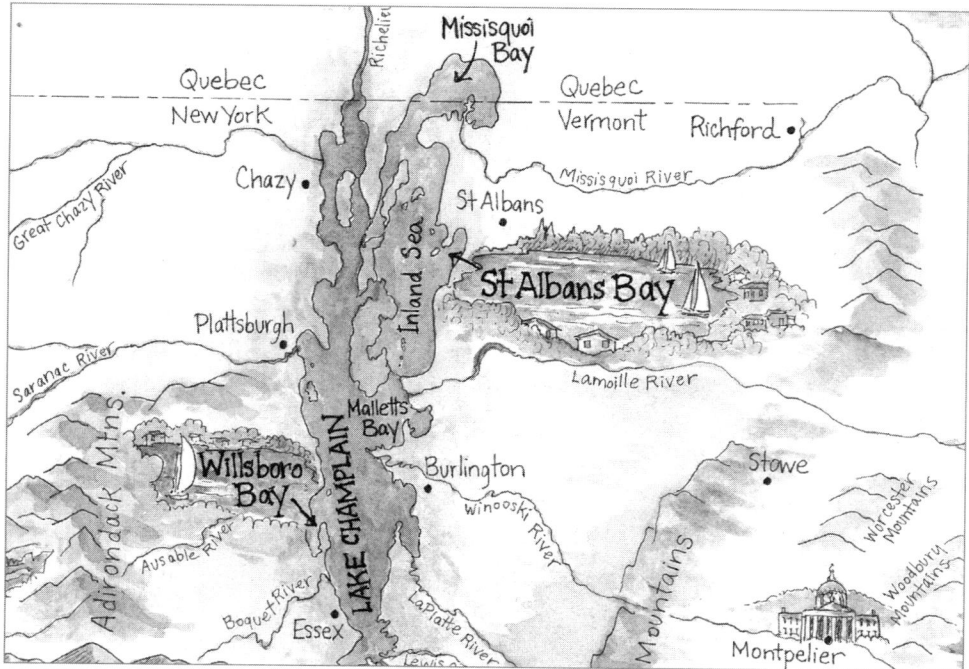

lakes in the flat Midwest than in the mountainous Adirondacks. The landscape around St. Albans Bay is relatively flat. As a result, every acre of the bay receives water from over seven acres of land. While this ratio is not particularly high compared to other sections of Lake Champlain, it is substantially higher than the ratio in Willsboro Bay, where each acre receives water from only about three acres of land.

The topography of the two catchments has guided development patterns as well. Not surprisingly, people find it easier to farm and settle in flat areas, so the St. Albans Bay basin is much more densely populated, containing a city of over 7,600 people and numerous farms. Meanwhile, steep mountains around Willsboro Bay have limited development, and there are only about 1,900 year-round residents.

The concentration of people and cows in the St. Albans Bay basin means more nutrients are produced. Through many years, the wastewater treatment facility for the City of St. Albans discharged very large amounts of nutrients into the bay, until an upgrade in 1987 resulted in substantial reductions. Agricultural sources in the drainage basin now account for the majority of nutrient loads. Unfortunately, efforts to minimize pollution from these sources have led to only marginal reductions. Over many years, the excess nutrients have built up in the bay's sediment and are slowly released each summer, adding to nutrients supplied annually from the basin.

The vast majority of Willsboro Bay's drainage basin is forested, and forest lands export few nutrients. There are relatively few agricultural acres in the basin, and the main population center in the area, the town of Willsboro, is oriented around the Boquet River, which does not even drain to the bay.

The superficial similarities in size between Willsboro Bay and St. Albans Bay are overwhelmed by underlying differences in their basins. Landscape and land use have combined to enhance accumulations of nutrients in the water of St. Albans Bay, and prevent such accumulation in Willsboro Bay. The nutrients combine with the shallower bay's warmer water to provide an ideal setting for annual irruptions of algae blooms. Thus far, Willsboro Bay has been spared such a fate, as London was spared the revolution that eventually engulfed Paris in Dickens's tale.

2

FORCES

Lakes are neither static nor isolated. They exchange materials and energy within themselves and between themselves and the surrounding drainage basin. Three critical forces that drive such exchanges are gravity, heat, and light. Gravity—exemplified by the journey of our four droplets in the previous chapter—has already been touched upon. The effects and interactions of heat and light also help define the physical environs of Lake Champlain.

◯ Retention Time

There was a period in my life when I never stayed in one place for more than a year. Attaching a post office box to my car would have been easier than dealing with all the change-of-address cards. Now I am married, have a child, own a house, and have been in the same town for five years. I know this town far better than any I passed through during my peripatetic days, though not nearly as well as our next-door neighbors do, after having been in their home over thirty years. The amount of time spent in any place affects water, just as it does people.

The average drop of water spends a little over two years in Lake Champlain. The retention time varies, depending on the lake segment considered. The large volume of the Main Lake takes the longest to change over—two and a half to three years. Water spends the least time in the South Lake—less than a month and a half. In between, the retention time is a little over three months for Missisquoi Bay, five to eight months for Malletts Bay, and nearly a year for the Inland Sea. Lake Champlain's overall retention time is similar to Lake Erie's, but by comparison water spends 191 years in Lake Superior.

The simplest calculation of retention time involves determining how long it would take in-flowing waters, under average conditions, to fill the volume of the water body in question if it were empty. Essentially, if you turned on a tap (in-flowing water) to fill a pot (the lake) how long would it take? The large volume of the Main Lake means that despite multiple large taps, it takes a long time to fill that huge pot. Meanwhile, though Malletts Bay has only one large tap—the Lamoille River—its pot is thirty times smaller than that of the Main Lake.

Water bodies that drain large catchments tend to refill more rapidly than those that drain small catchments. Large catchments tend to mean larger taps carrying more water. Lake Superior has a small catchment compared to its great volume, thus the long retention time.

Within any given neighborhood some individuals may choose to stay for many years, while others remain only six months; factors driving such decisions get lost when your perspective covers an entire city. Similarly, the rough calculations of retention time so far described omit many factors that affect the duration a given drop of water actually spends in a basin. Evaporation from and precipitation to the lake's surface are not included in the calculations. The significance of these factors would be greater on broad, shallow areas of the lake like Missisquoi Bay than it would be on narrower, deeper portions like the area between Thompson's Point and Split Rock.

On short time-scales, the extent of discharge at the outlet can affect retention time, by changing the volume of the pot. The Richelieu River limits the discharge of Lake Champlain during high-water events, increasing the volume of the lake instead. As a result, water entering during spring runoff may linger longer than water that comes in during a summer storm. The river narrows as it nears St-Jean, reducing the amount of water that can leave at any time. As a result the lake level remains high even after tributary levels have dropped.

On average the lake's level climbs almost three feet between the beginning of March and early May, peaking at about 99 feet above sea level. Flooding occurs at 100 feet. How high the lake gets before reaching its maximum depends on many factors. The amount of snow that accumulates through the winter is clearly important. Approximately 20 percent of annual precipitation falls between the beginning of December and the end of February, and much of it enters the lake only after melting. Spring temperatures are also critical. They affect not only how quickly that snow melts, but also how quickly the ground thaws. Frozen ground prevents new rains from percolating into the soil.

Although flooding is most prominent in the spring, this is not the period of greatest average precipitation. More rain falls during the three months of summer than in any other period, and autumn is slightly wetter than the spring. Yet late summer and fall is when the lake is lowest. By early October the lake usually stands at its lowest, about 95.2 feet above sea level. (The average lake level is about 95.8 feet, and nautical depth charts are based on a low lake level of 93.0 feet.)

Three factors prevent summer precipitation from having much of an effect on the lake. First, evaporation on long, hot days draws enormous quantities of water from the lake. Evaporation even accelerates as the days cool in the autumn, because the air above the lake is less humid. Second, plants throughout the drainage basin take up massive amounts of water to make food during the spring and summer. In fact, daily stream flow cycles during the growing season correlate closely with the sap production cycle of trees. Peak periods of sap production are followed in a few hours by minimum stream flows. Third, unlike during the winter, what water falls on land and is not taken up by plants can make its way slowly through the soil and become part of groundwater reserves. The lake continues to ebb until late-fall rains bring in more water than evaporation can take.

In addition to the effects of the lake level on retention time, deep and surface currents can move individual water molecules away from the discharge point or closer to it, and can even shunt sizable quantities of water between lake segments. A more complicated water budget would incorporate all these factors.

Retention time for water is not necessarily the same as retention time for other substances, though they are sometimes related. While water flows through a system, many pollutants do not. A few pollutants act like water in their ability to move in and out of the drainage basin. Chloride from road salt, for example, remains suspended in the water column; it does not react with other chemicals, and it does not precipitate. If loads from the drainage basin are constant, the chloride levels in the lake should also be constant. Thus increases in chloride in the lake likely reflect increased catchment inputs. On the other hand, phosphorus, an important plant and algae nutrient, settles into sediments or enters the food chain. The same is true of many toxic chemicals, such as mercury or PCBs.

Phosphorus levels are not completely independent of retention time. In lakes where the water moves quickly through the system, the phosphorus levels closely approximate those of the streams entering the lake. Lakes with longer retention times often have phosphorus levels lower than the streams feeding them because more phosphorus can settle out with the sediment. Some recent work has also tried to characterize how a lake's retention time influences the bacterial community that develops and how that might influence nutrient cycling, but results are not yet conclusive.

Retention in a community or lake carries benefits and drawbacks. In the community, the presence of longtime members means long-term memories and pride of place. At the same time, new members bring fresh ideas. In the lake, long retention times allow more nutrients like phosphorus to settle out from the in-flows; but lakes with shorter retention times can become clean faster if pollution inputs are reduced.

○ Catching a Wave

I can spend hours at the beach watching waves gently break against the shore. Few natural phenomena are as entrancing; only a campfire comes close. The eye is captivated by the repeating motion of water rushing ashore, creating different patterns in the sand with each swell. The crash of the surf or the rocking of a boat against a pier engages the ear. And the mind is freed to wander. My mind wanders to the phenomena of the waves themselves—what causes them, and why do they break?

On Lake Champlain it is generally easy to discern the cause of waves: the same wind that creates them is usually striking you in the face as you watch. On the ocean, however, the winds that create waves may be far offshore, making cause and effect much less obvious.

Still, the simple answer that wind causes waves begs the question of how. As air particles move in a certain direction, each particle at the interface with the water pushes on a particle of water due to friction. Water molecules bump into one another, thus propagating the phenomenon. The moving water molecules create ripples, which give texture to the lake surface. The increase in texture provides more surface area for the wind to push against and creates pockets of turbulence where still more energy can be transferred to the water. Eventually small ripples merge into waves.

Within each wave an individual water molecule moves up toward the crest of the wave and then down to the trough in a circular pattern. In deep water the molecules end up about where they started after the wave has passed; only the form of the wave moves on. In shallow water, however, both the molecules and the wave form move with the water molecules streaming up onto shore as the wave breaks, only to return immediately back into the lake.

The strength of the wind and how long it blows over the water determine the size of the waves. Two factors determine how long the wind blows over water—the duration of the storm, and the length of the water body, or fetch. From north to south Lake Champlain's fetch is about 120 miles, while from east to west it is only 12 miles at its maximum. That is why north-south winds will stir up substantially larger waves on Champlain than east-west winds.

Facing the wind on a beach offers the best opportunity to contemplate breaking waves. As the wave enters shallower water it slows, losing some of its energy of motion. However, since the wave is a transfer of energy from wind to water, and since energy cannot be created or destroyed, the energy of motion must be transferred. To accomplish this, the wave becomes taller, increasing its potential energy. Eventually, the tall wave above the water is moving faster than its foot dragging along the bottom, and the wave falls over. The water recedes back into the lake, but the energy is transferred to the land, causing erosion.

Energy is transferred to the land, causing erosion. (photo by Kevin Rose)

As waves approach shore they sometimes change directions and bend. I once sat on a small peninsula facing a sheltered cove while my back was to the lake. A motorboat passed on the lake. As the waves from the boat's wake hit the small peninsula, they bent around it until by the time they broke at my feet they were moving in the opposite direction from which they had started.

The boat's waves had been refracted around the peninsula because of shallower water there. The portion of the wave in the shallow water slowed, while the portion in deeper water continued at the same speed. Thus the faster portion of the wave wheeled around until both portions made landfall about head-on.

A sheltered bay between two points will receive less forceful wave action than the points themselves, because of wave refraction. Imagine a wave approaching such a shoreline. The points get hit first and absorb as much energy as the wave can deliver, but the remainder of the wave bends around the points. As it bends it stretches to land along the entire shoreline, and thus its energy is spread over a wider area. Erosion of the points can provide fine sediments that accumulate in the cove, forming beaches.

Unlocking the mysteries of waves does nothing to diminish their beauty. I am astounded by their ability to carve patterns in sand and rock. They, along with the pull of gravity and movement due to changes in density, are the principal means by which water moves on the lake. Now if I could only figure out why that campfire is so bewitching.

○ Autumn's Mix-up

Outside the night is a deep black, before 5 PM. Mist coats the windowpanes as the smells of cloves and nutmeg and cinnamon and apples from mulled cider fill the air. Tomorrow a thin coat of frost on the car window will require scraping, and I can rejoice in the symphonic crackle of dry leaves underfoot. Winter is near, and these are parts of the seasonal ritual.

Lake Champlain has its own late autumn ritual. Sometime in November or December those who spend time on the lake in quiet contemplation might notice the normally clear water become murky, despite the absence of rain. A stale, rotten smell may fill the air, even though the summer's algae blooms have long since passed. Lake Champlain will be in the midst of one of its twice-yearly mixings. The mixing, also called turnover, occurs when the water in a given section of the lake reaches near-uniform temperature from top to bottom for the first time since spring.

During the summer months the lake is layered, less dense and warm above, more dense and cool below, with a sharp transition, a thermocline, somewhere in the middle. As long as the upper, warm layer absorbs heat, the temperature and density differences between layers is accentuated. In addition to its temperature difference, the cool bottom layer has less oxygen. Fish and other creatures take oxygen from the deeper water, and because this layer is trapped below the warm layer above and not in contact with the air, the supply is never replenished.

Layering, or stratification, occurs when two conditions are met. First, if there isn't enough energy from the sun to warm the entire water body, layers form. This is typical of deep northern lakes, like Champlain, located where summers are short. Secondly, if the wind is not powerful enough to mix a lake's water from top to bottom, the water stratifies. Wind mixes shallow sections of the lake, like Missisquoi Bay, throughout the summer, preventing stratification.

The summer temperature of the cool lower layer is dependent upon the number of spring storms. Numerous spring storms provide lots of mixing, making the lower layer warmer; few spring storms mean less mixing and a cooler layer.

As autumn progresses, the waters of the lake give back to the air the warmth they had collected over the summer. The lake temperature becomes uniform from top to bottom, and the deep cold water returns to the surface, where it replenishes lost oxygen. Return of oxygen-starved water to the surface causes the stale, rotten smell. This mixing of deep and shallow layers happens at different times in different parts of the lake—earlier in shallower sections and later in the deepest portions.

Resurrection of the stagnant bottom waters is driven by two processes: wind and an increase in the density of the surface water. As the surface water surrenders its heat, the molecules pack closer together and begin to fall, much as cream will when added to a cup of hot coffee. Wind accelerates the process, like a spoon stirring the coffee. Sediments in the lake may be temporarily resuspended, like grounds in coffee, causing the murky appearance of the water.

One would expect cooling, increasing density, and subsequent falling of water to continue until the molecules locked together and became ice, but water acts differently from other compounds. Just above its freezing point, at about 39 degrees Fahrenheit, it begins to get less dense. The reasons are somewhat confusing and are usually glossed over in textbooks as being due to water's "unusual molecular constitution."

Anglers know that finding fish during the mixing period can be challenging. During the summer, fish congregate at the transition zone between the warm and cold layer. By doing so they stay deep enough to take advantage of cool temperatures and any detritus that floats down from above, without going so deep that low oxygen levels limit their activity. Once that transition zone disappears, fish disperse throughout the water column, and so their location is less predictable.

The length of the mixing period and the degree of mixing that occurs depend upon the weather. A rapid winter freeze shortens the autumn mixing period. Prior to freezing, the lake is highly unstable, and even a slight breeze can thoroughly stir the water. More wind and storms means more mixing.

Once the lake freezes over, it is again layered, this time with colder water—ice—over warmer water. Cold-over-warm layering persists until spring ice-out, when a second seasonal mixing occurs. Surface water absorbs heat until it is warmer than 39 degrees Fahrenheit and summer warm-over-cold layering is reestablished until late autumn or early winter.

So what happens if Lake Champlain doesn't freeze over? Then there is only one mixing per year, but it occurs throughout the winter. Such a situation is typical for very deep, narrow lakes like Cayuga and Seneca in New York, and for some of the Great Lakes, particularly Superior, Michigan, and Huron. In recent years it has become more common on Lake Champlain, because winter temperatures have been higher than average.

○ Slosh, Slosh

Summer stratification leads to autumn's mix-up, but density and temperature differences can interact with wind-driven waves to generate some hidden currents in the lake, like an internal seiche.

One gorgeous July day the lake called me incessantly. The air was hot and still. Over the weekend the water temperature had neared 70 degrees Fahrenheit. Expecting warm bathwater, I jumped into Kingsland Bay, only to find the water markedly colder than it had been just a day earlier. The swim was refreshing, but abbreviated. I had observed a hidden effect of the internal seiche, an example of what can happen to water when wind pushing on it overwhelms some of gravity's pulling effect.

Wind pushes water. The energy of the wind is transferred to the water, and waves rise. Waves of different sizes move at different speeds, so they start both to augment and to interfere with one another. Large waves can rise too high and then topple, creating whitecaps. Eventually, the waves expend their energy by crashing against the shore. With the smallest waves (less than three-quarters of an inch in length), the attraction of water molecules to one another pulls the surface back to a placid state. With larger waves, gravity provides the calming force.

When the wind is sufficiently strong, it pushes water to one end of the lake, as waves pile atop one another. A strong, constant wind of thirty miles per hour blowing along the long axis of the lake would create a pile less than a foot high—not exactly a towering tsunami. However, once the wind relaxes, that one foot of extra water sloshes back toward the other end. Sloshing continues, back and forth, until gravity pulls the water flat once again—a process that takes about four hours. The back-and-forth sloshing, known as a surface seiche, can reverse currents through some of the more constricted areas of the lake, like the Gut.

In order for the waves that induce the surface seiche to be created on the lake, there must be a difference in density between a moving medium and an otherwise stagnant medium. Wind—air in motion—represents the moving medium. Water, denser and more viscous, represents the stagnant medium. Currents produced by the surface seiche rarely influence water more than fifteen feet deep. By that depth, the density and inertia of the water have absorbed the excess energy of the wind push. However, the thermocline provides another area in the lake where media of different densities lie in contact.

A swimmer diving through the water column will come across an area where the temperature drops quickly—the thermocline. A temperature difference also indicates a density difference, with the warm top layer being slightly less dense than the cold deeper layer. These differences become accentuated as warming continues through spring and summer. The thermocline develops most clearly in the Main Lake and Malletts Bay.

The Inland Sea hosts a thermocline, but it is less distinct than in deeper segments. Wind thoroughly mixes shallower lake sections like Missisquoi Bay and the South Lake, so they often retain a uniform top-to-bottom temperature.

The piling of waves on one end of the lake that creates the surface seiche also generates downward pressure on the thermocline—the start of an explanation for the quick change in water

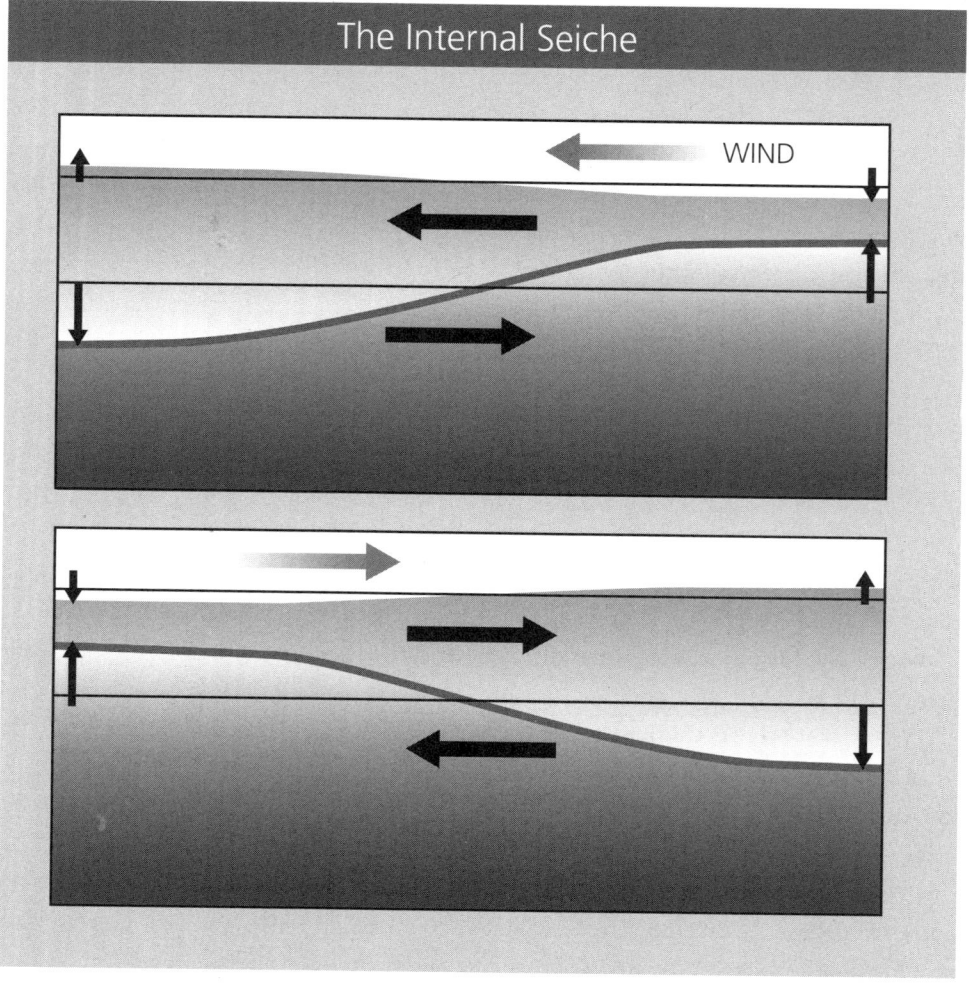

Wind forces water to accumulate at one end of the lake, generating a downward pressure on the thermocline and creating an internal seiche wave that travels toward the opposite end of the lake (top). As the wind dies and the internal wave reaches the opposite end of the lake, the direction of travel reverses (bottom). (diagram from Tom Manley)

temperature observed that day at Kingsland Bay. Due to the relatively small difference in density between the layers above and below the thermocline, just a small downward pressure creates a very large wave. Imagine how much a water-bed mattress sags beneath you when you flop upon it, compared to a denser wooden board.

Once induced, this large underwater wave, an internal seiche, sloshes back and forth from north to south (with a bit of east-west rocking) throughout the summer. Though the conditions that established the internal seiche may have disappeared, the currents once set in motion continue. It takes four to six days for a wave to complete the trip. The thermocline rises at one end of the lake on day one and at the other end on day three. In between it flattens. At Kingsland Bay I had experienced the rise of the thermocline to near the water surface. By the next day, the swim would once again resemble bathwater as the thermocline fell back.

The internal seiche represents perhaps the greatest mixing force in the lake. It can displace the thermocline as much as 145 feet. Middlebury College researcher Tom Manley has suggested that over 25 percent of the water in the Main Lake shifts with the passage of an internal seiche wave. It can create currents in excess of one mile per hour—one hundred times faster than the average north-south current. While largely restricted to the Main Lake, it has been detected reaching south beyond the Crown Point Bridge. The internal seiche causes substantial exchange of energy and materials throughout the lake, all created by the simple push of wind against water and the transfer of that force to lower depths.

○ Let There Be Light

In February I begin to notice the return of the sun. Through late autumn and early winter, the onset of darkness signaled that it was time to begin thinking of heading home from work. Gradually, as the year progresses, not only my workday but also the commute home is illuminated by sunlight. All of a sudden skiers yearn for a final snowstorm so they can take advantage of the long spring days. People's moods improve as winter layers are shed. And, of course, the lake responds.

Though we notice the lengthening of days, the increasing angle of the sun is a more important (though closely related) factor that warms Lake Champlain. When the sun shines from a higher angle above the horizon, the intensity of heat reaching a given surface area increases. The angle of the sun varies with the time of day, the season, and the latitude of a lake. On Champlain, the angle of the sun reaches its peak at midday during the summer.

It is easy to demonstrate the effects of light angle on energy intensity. Shine a flashlight on a piece of paper and trace the area illuminated. As you vary the angle of the flashlight from directly above the paper to the side, while keeping its distance constant, the area of the paper illuminated stretches and grows. Since the intensity of the light has not changed, each unit area of the paper must receive less energy.

With increasing daylight, the heat budget of Lake Champlain shifts. After long nights of radiating heat to the atmosphere, the lake begins absorbing energy. The exact time of switch in any given year depends on the frigidity of the winter and the number of cloudy days where sunlight is scattered and therefore less intense.

However, the period when the lake is warmest or coldest does not coincide with the highest and lowest periods of available sunlight. Lake Champlain receives the least light during the December winter solstice, but has the least energy at the end of February or early March. Between December and the end of winter the lake continues to lose more energy to cold and night than it gains from sunlight. The most light is available during the June solstice, but the lake contains the most heat energy in early August, because it continues to soak up sun during the long, hot summer days.

The lag between maximum light and maximum heat in the lake allows a predictable change in dominance of algae species

Storm clouds and sunset (photo by Carolyn L. Bates)

through a season. Some species, diatoms in particular, respond to the increasing spring light levels and dominate early in the year. Diatom blooms have been recorded even when lakes are still ice-covered. Abundant nutrients further aid early spring algae. Rivers continue to carry nutrients into the lake throughout the winter, but there is less assimilation of the nutrients until light becomes more available. Blue-green algae are more competitive at higher temperatures, and thus they dominate in the late summer. Some blue-greens also make use of atmospheric nitrogen when in-lake sources might be low (having been tied up by the earlier-growing species), thus gaining another late-summer advantage.

The clarity of the water through which light passes affects the amount of space where algae can survive. As light moves through a water column, it is absorbed and scattered by various particles, including decaying plant matter, suspended clay particles, and algae themselves. Thus the intensity of the light is diminished, and when the intensity drops below 0.5 to 1 percent of what's available at the surface, photosynthesis cannot occur. In Lake Champlain the water tends to be clearest in the Main Lake, where on average during the summer sufficient light might penetrate thirty-five to fifty-five feet. Water is cloudiest in the most southern portions of the lake, where light limits photosynthesis below about nine feet in depth. Together light and heat are the two critical drivers of a lake's physical and biological processes.

○ Lake Ice

"It's freezing!" my wife exclaimed coming in from a short walk. Such a strange phrase to my too-literal ear. Was she benignly describing the weather, or commenting upon an actual process occurring? I knew if I asked the question it would elicit only a scowl. On this evening she could have meant both, as temperatures plunged, stars twinkled, and the air was still.

Clear, cold, windless nights present ideal conditions for the actual freezing of ponds and lakes. Clear skies mean no cloud-cover blanket to trap heat radiated away from the earth overnight. Colder air allows more heat to be transferred from the water. Absence of wind means that once the ice begins to form, wave action stirred by the wind will not interrupt the process.

Different bodies of water freeze at different times, and three of the principal factors influencing which lakes freeze and which do not are the lake's location, volume, and area. Obviously a lake in Florida is less likely to freeze than a lake in the Northeast, but the other aspect of location is altitude. Colder temperatures at higher elevations make lakes in the mountains more likely to freeze. Volume is another relatively obvious factor. It takes more time and colder air temperatures to draw the heat out of a large volume of water than it does for a small volume of water. For that reason, fairly small lakes that are very deep take much longer to freeze. The influence of lake area is a little less obvious, but the expanse of a flat, treeless surface provides no hindrance to gathering winds, which can break up the ice as it forms. Thus, large lakes freeze more slowly than small lakes of a similar volume.

Freezing in very large lakes is usually preceded by a few good snowstorms. When snow lands in the lake, it warms and changes from a solid to a liquid form of water. Such a transformation requires more energy than does a commensurate change in temperature without a change in phase. Thus the snow saps more of the lake's energy reserves, facilitating a freeze-over.

A frozen lake allows winter recreation—ice-skating, ice boating, or in my case slipping and falling. For many people, zipping around on ice skates with fresh, cold air stinging cheeks seems an idyllic pastime. To me, being on ice skates simply means I am a few inches farther away from the slippery hard surface. Inevitably, the skates slide out from under me, and my arms and legs flail like a cartoon character's. However, just before achieving a full seated position, I have an opportunity to wonder, "What makes ice so darn slippery?"

Conventional wisdom holds that the pressure exerted by a person standing on the very narrow surface area of the skate blade melts a thin layer of ice, thus reducing the friction between the skater and the surface. Unfortunately, the laws of nature confound conventional wisdom. If this hypothesis were true, the fastest speed skaters should be built like football linemen, because they would concentrate more weight on the same area.

While it is true that an increase in pressure decreases the melting point of ice, an average hockey player would exert only enough pressure to lower the melting point by a few tenths of a degree. Whatever benefit excess melting conveys quickly disappears as the temperature drops. On the contrary, however, colder temperatures (to a point) produce faster ice.

Friction appears to be more important for melting ice than the downward pressure from the skater. Friction occurs because the ice surface resists the movement of the skate over it; the resistance generates heat; and the heat causes a thin layer of melting. But even friction doesn't fully explain the slipperiness of ice.

At the surface of ice is a thin "quasi-liquid" layer that forms because the water molecules at the surface do not have other water molecules to bond to on one side. The molecules want to hang out with the "cool" folks in the ice lattice but just cannot find enough partners to make them stick around. Unlike a true liquid, where molecules would vibrate and move in all directions, molecules in the quasi-liquid layer vibrate only up and down. Apparently the quasi-liquid layer is responsible for the slipperiness of ice, though the exact mechanisms are not entirely clear.

At the surface of the ice is a thin "quasi-liquid" layer. (photo by Trip Kinney)

This layer exists at temperatures as low as minus 250 degrees Fahrenheit, where it is only a few molecules wide, and becomes thickest just before the ice enters a true liquid state. The thicker the layer, the more resistance it gives skates, but the softer it makes landings when the skates slip out from under you.

Once I am flat on my back, massaging the elbow that took the brunt of my last fall, I ponder, "Why is ice so darn hard?" After all, snow is also frozen water, but I would much rather fall into a snowdrift than onto an ice-covered lake.

When water molecules cool enough to form ice, each molecule attaches to four other molecules, forming a rigid lattice structure. The basic structural unit is repeated as long as there are neighboring water molecules. Snowflakes are loosely bound aggregations of such crystals. In the atmosphere, where snow forms, molecules eventually run out of neighbors to join. In a lake, finding neighboring water molecules does not present a challenge.

Thus, though snowflakes are technically ice, they are not chemically connected to one another. The ice in a lake, on the other hand, forms one massive lattice. In a snowdrift, the energy of a falling body can be used to push the particles away from one another, while the rigidity of ice's lattice prevents molecules from separating in lake ice. If, however, the downward force of a falling (or even stationary) object exceeds the ability of the ice lattice to exert a counterforce, the lattice breaks and the object goes plunging into the frigid water below.

How does one know when the ice is thick enough so that you avoid such a plunge? As a general guide, four inches of clear solid ice can easily support someone with an adequate margin of safety, but my rule of thumb is to wait until you've seen someone else (or better yet, someone else's vehicle) on the ice before heading out. Honestly, ice is never completely safe; there are always areas that will be thinner. Furthermore, strength depends not only on thickness, but also snow cover, depth of water under the ice, size of the water body, chemistry of the ice, currents, distribution of load on the ice, and other factors.

Two different types of ice cover can form on the lake, depending on conditions at the time of freezing. Ice formation can be rapid, with as much as five miles of ice forming in only fifteen minutes. When a skin of ice forms all at once like this and then continues to grow from the initial start, it is called sheet ice. Sheet ice tends to be smooth and relatively homogeneous, though cracks will appear. Alternatively, separate masses of ice can fuse together, forming agglomeritic ice. Agglomeritic ice can result, for example, when wave action or other turbulence prevents a continuous sheet from forming but it is so cold that freezing occurs anyway, or when sheet ice breaks up and then re-forms.

The sheet of ice over a lake is not static; it continues to grow, shrink, and move throughout the winter. Though ice is less dense than the water beneath, it is still subject to normal expansion and contraction with further changes in temperature. Three phenomena that demonstrate the dynamic nature of ice are pressure ridges, tension cracks, and ice ramparts.

Each of these three phenomena result from the expansion of ice as it warms. Pressure ridges result from the buckling of ice as it expands. Eventually the buckling leads to cracks, and one sheet of ice shoots up over another. The cracks form at right angles to the movement of the expanding ice, in a process similar to how mountains form. In contrast to pressure ridges, tension cracks form when ice molecules pull apart. As ice expands, molecules already locked within the ice lattice pull away from one another, creating tension. The addition of even a slight amount of pressure, such as from a walking person, can relieve the tension and allow a thin fissure to appear, usually accompanied by a loud snap. Ice ramparts form when the expanding sheet of ice pushes against the shoreline rather than against more ice. The pressure from the expanding ice can force gravel and stones onto the land. Ice ramparts can cause severe damage to shoreline property or to docks that may have been left in the water.

Though ice ramparts provide a mechanism for moving sand and gravel toward shore during the winter, anchor ice can move them in the opposite direction. Anchor ice is ice that attaches to the bottom of a lake or river. As it forms, it adheres to sediment and pebbles. When the ice breaks free of the bottom, it can lift and transport the sediment wherever the raft of ice floats. A similar process was responsible for moving large quantities of soil and stone to different parts of the Champlain Valley after the glaciers melted. One study on Lake Michigan suggests anchor ice is responsible for removing 9.1 cubic feet of sand from each foot of beach!

○ Understanding Your River

Ice is not nearly as effective at moving materials to the lake as are the rivers that flow to it. Not only do rivers shape the landscape, they also provide the nutrients that drive the lake's food web, and the sediment that will in the long run fill the lake.

At the summer camp where I used to work, there was a dependable little trickle of groundwater at the east end of the beach that flowed over the sand and into the lake. This area was a favorite haunt of the younger campers, and throughout the summer it would be festooned with castles, moats, tiny ponds, and channels. On no two days was the path of the trickle over the beach the same. I too spent some of my free time there playing in the sand.

Tyler Branch, Franklin County, Vermont (photo by Mike Winslow)

I particularly enjoyed pouring bucket after bucket of water into a small pond dug in the beach. The pond would overflow and carve a valley through the sand as its water raced toward the lake. Before long a delta would form as my river fanned out when the topography flattened at the water's edge. Upstream the rivulet would carve a deep gorge. Bends appeared until the water undercut a bank; the bank would collapse and create an island. Adding obstructions like rocks or twigs to a bank might stabilize it, but other portions of the river would change in seemingly unpredictable ways.

Four key variables drive the evolution of a river's shape over time: the size of sediment particles, the quantity of sediment, the amount of water in the stream, and the slope of the stream. A change in any one of these factors triggers compensating adjustments in one or more of the others, with changes in the size or quantity of sediment proportional to changes in volume of water or slope. For example, if heavy rains swell the river, increasing its volume, then it will pluck more and larger sediment from its bed and banks. Increases in the amount of sediment carried will also occur if the river cuts off a meander bend, which increases the slope because the channel now traverses the same elevation over a shorter distance. On the other hand, if the volume of water decreases due to a drought or upstream beaver dam, the river deposits more sediment, rather than carrying it. When the river starts to meander around deposited sediment piles, then its slope decreases.

Changes in my play river occurred quickly and dramatically because the water on the beach passed through sand, a notoriously unstable medium. Nevertheless, the situation is analogous to what happens on real rivers; well-intentioned actions along one stretch may have unintended consequences in another. For example, I know a tributary to the Missisquoi River where a house sits poised just a few feet from a steep sandbank overlooking the water. When I was last there, a fallen tree in the river below, root mass still attached and leaves still green, offered testimony that, not very long ago, the precipice had not been so close to the house. Year after year the river has expended its energy eating at the bank, inching closer and closer to the home.

Generally, the river is not characterized by such high eroding banks. Part of it meanders lazily through farm fields. Other sections plunge madly through confined rocky chasms. At this site, however, the river acts as if it is in a rocky chasm while the surrounding landscape is gentle farmland. So why does the river not fit the landscape?

Throughout the Lake Champlain basin, river managers have begun to realize the importance of comprehensive evaluations of rivers—their present condition and likely future responses to change—in order to answer such questions. These studies, called geomorphic assessments, begin with an examination of the present condition of the river based on maps and existing data. How has the river responded to the topography over which it flows? How wide or narrow is it? How and where has it been modified? If it has been modified, how does its current appearance compare to that of unmodified rivers passing over similar topography? By means of computer software, electronic versions of maps can be laid over one another so that information on all the maps can be compiled in one form.

A geomorphic assessment looks at the whole river, rather than just the uncharacteristic parts, and tries to link anomalous situations—like the steep eroding bank beneath the house—in one section to changes in another area. Wide pools may appear where one would expect steep cascades, or straight channels where the landscape suggests exploratory meanders. In the first step of an assessment, the river analyst identifies discernible pieces of the river, called reaches. Borders between different reaches are defined by variations in the physical setting, such as a change in slope, valley width, or soil type. Such landscape features are a good predictor of how a river will appear if there has not been any artificial modification. Steep, rocky gorges create rigid boundaries through which the waters race with wild abandon, while broad, gentle terrain allows the river to spread out.

Causes of deviation are sometimes obvious. A dam may lead to reduced amounts of water and sediment moving through the stream below the dam. Meanders may have been channelized to prevent localized flooding. Riverbanks may be armored with large rocks to prevent erosion. The rocks are too large for the river to carry, but since the slope and water volume remain unchanged, erosion will still occur, just in a different place.

Less obvious causes can include changes in use of the surrounding land. An increase in developed land, for example, would mean more water flows through the same channel in a shorter period of time, because of increased storm runoff from roads and rooftops. Bridges and culverts constrain the river by making it move through a certain point, preventing its natural inclination to wander. The river begins to act like a snake in your hand, thrashing wildly back and forth wherever it is not confined by your grip.

Past events frequently provoke present-day problems. For example, the eroding sandbank below the house absorbs the energy of 2,000 feet of straightened channel. The river upstream had meandered through a relatively flat valley, but at some point in the past it was channelized by a farmer trying to protect his cropland from flooding. The resulting increase in slope led to the river's grabbing additional sediment from the bank below the imperiled house.

When the river's adjustment process conflicts with human investments, analysis through geomorphic assessment helps suggest appropriate solutions that do not compromise the overall river basin. In the case of the house, that could mean restoring upstream meanders or moving the house farther from the river. Implementation of river management tools in the absence of watershed analysis often leads to money and energy wasted on improper solutions. For example, armoring a crumbling stream bank with rock may halt erosion in one place, but the erosion will likely be transferred to another stream reach. Dredging a river can cause later erosion upstream and downstream of the point where gravel or sediment was removed.

In a way, the process of understanding rivers is similar to understanding people. In both cases, you need to analyze the whole being—past, present, and future expectations—in order to alleviate and prevent problem behaviors.

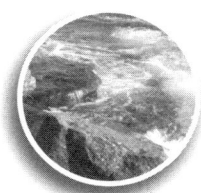

3
PHENOMENA

Lake Champlain holds many secrets and mysteries and just plain odd happenings. This chapter explores six such phenomena that many might recognize but few will have given a second thought. The first five are accessible to anyone who spends time on the lake. The sixth appears on the lake bottom.

○ Thick Frothy Foam

At the end of my workday I often take time to contemplate the rich frothy head of a cold beer. Why is it that, on a beer, foam is associated with cleanliness and a superior product, while on a lake foam is considered by many to be an indicator of pollution?

The processes by which foam is created in the two instances are similar, requiring two events. First, there must be a reduction in the natural surface tension of the water. Surface tension describes the competing forces acting on molecules at the interface between liquid and air—molecules caught between two worlds. Surface tension allows water striders to stride and spring pollen to float. Second, air must be mixed into the water, forming bubbles.

Reduction of surface tension occurs whenever there are molecules that congregate and act at the surface of the liquid. These "surface active" molecules are dubbed surfactants, for short. Chemical companies spend a great deal of time and money developing surfactants for use in cleaning detergents. In beer, proteins from the barley and hops act as surfactants. In lake and river water, particles leached from decaying plant matter and soil are naturally occurring surfactants. Surface tension in natural water systems can vary remarkably from place to place. It is highest in clear water and lower in colored water (the color usually being caused by substances that can act as surfactants). It is also lower in the immediate vicinity of plants, suggesting that even when alive, plants exude surfactants.

The process of mixing air with liquid in beer is somewhat different from what happens in lakes. In beer, the carbon dioxide naturally occurring in the product is released as the liquid is poured. Scratches and irregularities in the glass become focal points for the collection of gas bubbles. In lakes there are many mechanisms by which air can be added to the water. Windy days create crashing waves that trap air. Heating of stagnant water reduces its ability to hold gases, which thus leave solution. On rivers foam forms in rapids and near falls as water crashes over rocks.

Once the air has been mixed into the water, bubbles form. The bubbles are a thin film of water around pockets of air. Surfactants provide a rigid structure to which the water molecules adhere. The size of the bubbles formed greatly influences the appearance and properties of the foam. Compare for instance a heavy beer like a stout, which typically has very small bubbles, with the larger bubbles of a pilsner.

Today, you can expect a natural cause when you see foam on a lake, but that was not always the case. Detergents on the market in the 1950s and '60s did not break down as readily as most detergents sold today do, so they built up in the water, intensifying production of naturally occurring foam. This, combined with the regular appearance of natural foams in areas with high concentrations of decaying plants, explains why foam on water is often associated with pollution. Meanwhile, the foam in the beer is associated with cleanliness because any oils or detergents that haven't been rinsed from the glass will cause the foam to disappear more quickly.

Windy days create crashing waves that trap air. (photo by Kevin Rose)

Naturally occurring foams in water differ from foams that would indicate pollution. Naturally occurring foams often have a tannish or brownish color and smell earthy or fishy. Detergent foams are whiter and often smell of perfume.

Occasionally foam production can still be traced back to pollution sources. Such foams are most likely to occur near outfalls from storm sewers. A particularly common culprit is car washing. To maximally protect water quality when washing cars, do so over lawns or other pervious surfaces to prevent the detergents from running directly into storm sewers. Alternatively, use a commercial car wash.

Over time foam dissipates. Gas diffuses from one bubble to another, and in the process the film of liquid sometimes bursts, merging the bubbles. Additionally, the water in the foam is pulled downward by gravity, leaving drier, larger bubbles on top. With less water, these bubbles are weaker. Thus, both the frothy mess on the beach and the rich creamy head in my beer will disappear.

○ Streaking

Anyone who has been boating on Lake Champlain at just the right time can observe long parallel streaks of foam and perhaps debris stretched out along the water. They appear during breezes of between six and fifteen miles per hour. If a stronger wind blows—for example one that stretches a light flag—the streaks become nearly impossible to observe as waves disrupt them. The streaks are visible manifestations of a series of temporary counterspinning surface currents referred to as Langmuir circulation.

Picture an old-fashioned laundry wringer, with one cylinder revolving clockwise and the other counterclockwise. The cylinders represent cells of the current, but where the wringer has only two cylinders, there can be many more Langmuir cells operating in pairs. The wringers orient almost parallel to the wind, meaning currents are perpendicular to the waves. Down-welling currents occur at the surface where wringers come together, and upwelling areas where adjacent cells come together below the surface. Streaks form at the areas of down-welling because the natural buoyancy of any foam and plankton already at the surface resists the downward current.

The distance between streaks is determined by the size of the wringers, which is in turn determined by the depth of the thermocline. A wringer will reach down to the point of rapid temperature transition between warm surface waters and cold depths of the lake. Streaks are close together during early spring and late fall because the thermocline is relatively shallow. As the summer sun warms the lake water, the thermocline becomes deeper, and any streaks that form sit farther apart.

The circulation pattern was named for Irving Langmuir, an industrial engineer and Nobel laureate who first described the phenomenon in 1938. He had noticed the streaks during an earlier trans-Atlantic voyage and set about describing their formation while on vacation in Lake George in the Champlain basin.

Langmuir accurately described the currents that generate the streaks, but the cause of the currents themselves is still the subject of some debate. Apparently, as the wind moves over the water, shear forces cause a surface current at a slight angle to the wind. The surface layer causes the layer beneath it to move as well. However, the force exerted by the surface layer on the layer beneath is less than the force exerted by the wind on the surface layer. The resulting drag causes the current to shift, directed by the wind, until it is perpendicular.

Understanding Langmuir circulation increases our ability to understand the biology of the lake. Because of the Langmuir circulation, plankton are not randomly

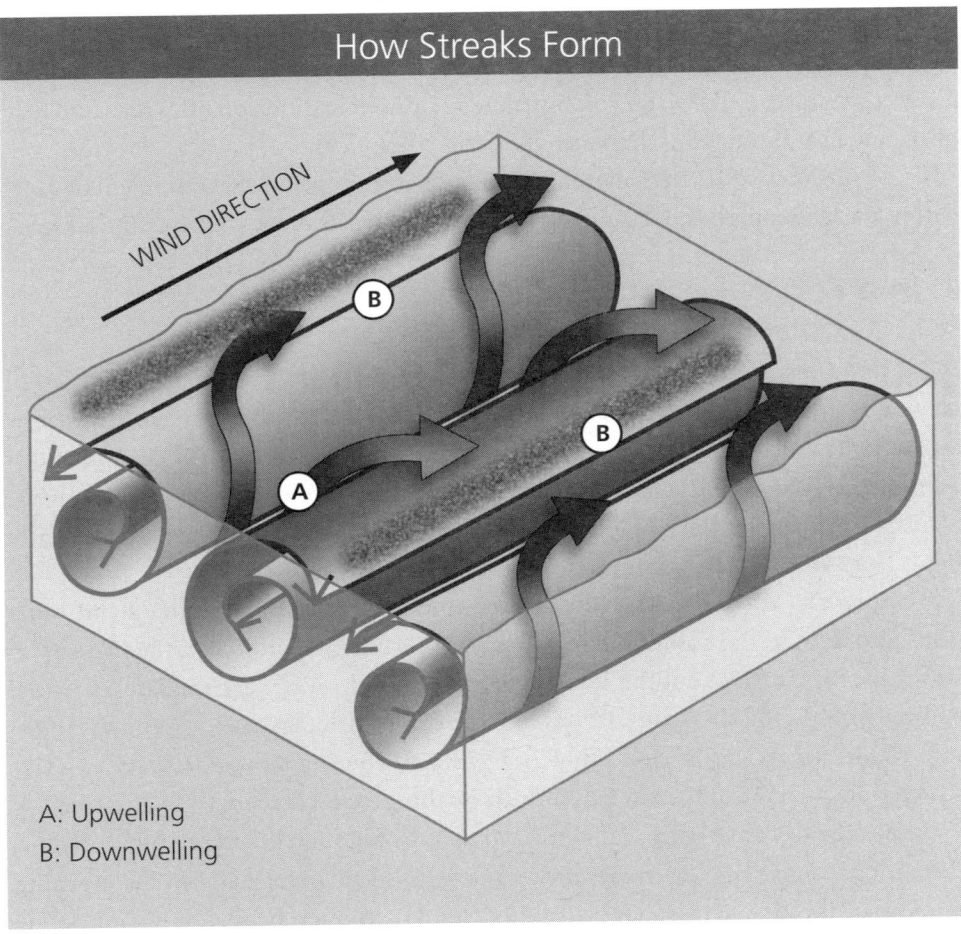

Langmuir currents orient parallel to the wind. Streaks form at the areas of downwelling.

distributed, but concentrated in the streaks. Attempting to assess the number and diversity of plankton in the lake just by sampling in a streak would be akin to trying to estimate the population of the United States by sampling people only in New York City. Any study designed to measure plankton diversity must account for the potential patchy distribution of its subjects.

Organisms that live deep underwater may also be brought unwillingly toward the surface. For example, tiny larval flies called phantom midges use oxygen-poor deep waters to hide from fish. Studies in Finland have shown that these midges get trapped in the upwelling portions of Langmuir cells, because the currents are too fast for the midges to swim against. Midges congregate in underwater versions of the above-water streaks, resulting in a smorgasbord for the fish that feed upon them.

In addition to the effects on biota, Langmuir circulation influences the chemical and thermal properties of the water. Although the circulating cells probably become less distinct lower in the water column, they still promote diffusion of oxygen and help distribute heat throughout the water above the thermocline.

Like the internal seiche, Langmuir streaks demonstrate how the movement of water within the lake complicates a simplistic idea of how water moves through the lake.

○ In a Fog

It is not unusual for me to awake in a bit of a haze. I am not a morning person. I stumble about the house, eyes half open, and fiddle with the coffeemaker, eagerly awaiting the welcome drip of hot black liquid filling the carafe. Some mornings, however, the neighbor's house across the street can hardly be seen through a thick, white blanket. Cars pass by, their headlights barely penetrating the mist. The haze is not just in my head when a classic autumn fog settles around my house.

Fog results when the water in the air condenses onto dust particles and other water droplets. In the autumn, Lake Champlain is often warmer than the mass of air sitting over it. Throughout the evening, air closest to the water accumulates moisture and warmth. As the air warms, it rises into the colder, drier layer above, and the moisture condenses. Wisps of cloud flow heavenward, offering an opportunity to watch convection currents in the air. Fog formed by this process is referred to as steam fog. Typically, the day's sun warms all the air so that the fog soon burns off; but the colder the air mass above the water, the thicker the fog is likely to be. Later in the morning, as more of the air warms, a layer of fluffy clouds can often be seen hovering, seemingly suspended between the water and the otherwise azure blue sky.

On the night of October 11, 1776, what was likely a steam fog played a role in the daring escape of the American fleet from a larger British armada. Benedict Arnold and his hastily assembled squadron had spent much of the day battling the British off Valcour Island. The Americans had lost two of their ships, and another three were gravely damaged. The day had been marked by a northerly wind, and during the evening a thick fog settled. Knowing that his fleet would not survive another day of fighting, Arnold and his men sought escape. They muffled their oarlocks with shirts and slipped right past the British ships, hidden by the dark and fog. When the British commander, Guy Carleton, awoke on the morning of October 12, he was mortified to find his enemy had escaped undetected.

Carleton gave chase, eventually cornering his prey in Crescent Bay at the south end of Grand Isle—or so he thought. When the fog lifted, he found he had wasted the morning bombing a small rock island, which has ever since borne the name Carleton's

Carleton's Prize
(photo by
Carolyn L. Bates)

Prize. Meanwhile Arnold had escaped to the south, eventually landing the remnant of his ragtag fleet at what is now called Arnold's Bay.

The cooling of already moist air causes other types of fog, such as radiation fog, valley fog, up-slope fog, and advection fog.

Radiation fog may develop at any time of year, but it is most pronounced in late fall and early winter, promoted by long nights and a dry upper atmosphere. On clear, calm nights, the surface of the earth cools through the night, and warmer air above it comes closer and closer to its dew point, until radiation fog develops. Absence of wind prevents vertical mixing of the air, so the layer nearest the earth cools the most. Like steam fog, radiation fog usually burns off with morning sunlight.

Frequently, weather reports will predict patchy valley fog. Valley fog forms via the same mechanism as radiation fog, but cold air falling into valleys can cause this type of fog to become extremely thick. Shading from mountains inhibits the sun's ability to burn off valley fog.

At higher elevations, up-slope fog forms fairly regularly. As warm, moist air rises up the Adirondack or Green Mountains, it cools to the point where the water it is carrying condenses. Up-slope fog is usually thickest when I am hiking in the High Peaks to view fall foliage.

The poet Carl Sandburg once described fog as coming on "little cat feet." He was probably watching advection fog creep quietly into Chicago, the city where he lived for many years. Advection fog forms when warm, moist air is blown over a colder surface until it cools to the dew point. While wind serves to dissipate radiation fog, advection fog depends on it. Advection fog is very common in San Francisco, where a cold-water current runs just offshore. It also occurs when a warm air mass moves in over late-winter snows. Once it forms, advection fog can be more difficult to burn off than radiation or steam fog.

Valley fog (photo by Mark H. Snelling)

When commuting to work on socked-in days, I eventually get to a place where the road gains just enough elevation to rise above the dense fog and offers an opportunity to admire the billowing white clouds filling the valley below. The mental haze that started my morning subsides as my caffeine fix takes hold. Similarly, as the sun's rays grow stronger, the fog below quickly burns off, yielding to another bright, sunny autumn day.

○ Mirages

January 10, 2007: Crossing the causeway between Grand Isle and the mainland of Vermont I noticed something odd to the north: a bank of white with trees floating above in the area just north of Sand Bar State Park. A similar, though less distinct phenomenon could also be viewed to the south where the old railroad causeway separated Malletts Bay from the Main Lake. It had snowed earlier in the day, but the sky was clear as I crossed. It was afternoon, an odd time for fog, which usually develops overnight and burns off early. Besides, if snow or fog were causing this phenomenon, either the trees would be in and out of drifts, or completely invisible. Instead, I was viewing a particularly strong version of an optical illusion.

Some relevant facts may help explain the phenomenon I witnessed. The winter had been exceedingly warm, and, just a few days before, daily high temperatures had reached into the 60s, shattering all previous records. As a result, lake water temperatures, at about 40 degrees Fahrenheit, were higher than average for this time of year. However, just that morning, winter weather had moved into the area, and air temperatures at the time of the mirage were around 20 degrees Fahrenheit.

Optical illusions such as these occur when there are sharp differences in air temperature. Light bends toward the cooler, denser layer of air. In this case, a warm layer of air sat between the lake and the cooler upper atmosphere, and the light entering my eye had not traveled a straight line from its source. However, my mind interpreted the light as having traveled a straight line, and therefore placed the image generated on a straight path, at the water surface. Thus I was viewing the white clouds of the sky in a place where they were not. Meanwhile, the light from the trees had not passed between the two layers of different temperature air, so my mind correctly interpreted their location.

The mirage created has a more widely recognized form. On very hot days while traveling along the highway, it is common to see shimmering "water" in the road ahead. The "water" is actually an image of the blue sky that appears in the wrong place because light has been bent as it passed through the superheated air at the road surface.

Both my floating trees and the water in the roadway are known as inferior mirages. The image one views is located below, or inferior to, its actual position. For inferior mirages to occur, there must be at least a 3-degree-Fahrenheit difference in temperature between the surface layer of air and higher-elevation air, and the mirages are stronger the greater the difference in temperature. Thus, the nearly 20-degree-Fahrenheit difference on this day had produced a particularly strong image.

One may also occasionally witness superior mirages on Lake Champlain. Superior mirages occur when the layer of air above is warmer than the layer below. In springtime, warm air masses may move over the lake, while the water retains winter's chill. Superior mirages can take on different forms. When the difference in temperature between the ground layer and the air is very high, the mirage may float in the sky upside down above the actual object. In these cases, even if the object is beyond the horizon, the mirage may still be visible. Such superior mirages may account for many sightings of UFOs, where headlights from distant cars become visible for a brief moment before disappearing. When the temperature differential between the two air layers is not so great, distant objects simply appear elongated.

Occasionally, a superior image, known as a hillingar, or arctic mirage, might appear. When the temperature differential between the colder air over the water and the warmer air above exceeds 10 degrees Fahrenheit per 100 feet in elevation, the horizon appears as if it were turned upward. Bob Tendy describes such an image seen from his family's cabin in Crown Point: "the entire Vermont shoreline [about a mile away] seems to be only about 20–30 yards away. The magnification is always the same, the view is always the same, and to the right of the cabin there always appears to be a huge island which sits only a short swim away. I have always seen this in the early morning, usually beginning at about 4 AM, and it disappears by 5. But if there is a good moon, I can see it earlier. I have always seen it in the summer, though I have seen less magnificent versions of it at other times of the year."

One particularly poetic version of a superior mirage is referred to as fata morgana. Here, distant objects are greatly elongated and seem to form turrets like those of a distant castle stretching into the sky while simultaneously plunging into the depths of the water. The mirage draws its name from the legendary Morgan Le Fay, half sister of King Arthur. Morgan possessed the power of the fairies, and the mirage purportedly represents her magical home. This particular mirage requires three layers of air—a very cold one near the surface, a thin layer of warmer air, and then another cold layer above. The image of any objects seen through the thin middle layer of air becomes greatly magnified. As the layers shift due to turbulence and minor spatial variations, the mirage stretches, retracts, and shimmers, adding to the overall effect of the mirage.

Pay close attention to those distant objects on the horizon when you are on the lake. Maybe you, too, will be able to see floating trees, distant upside-down boats, exceedingly tall cliffs, looming shorelines, or perhaps a sea serpent that can best be explained as a mirage.

○ Let It Snow

Snow. Ski areas depend on it. Retirees flee from it. It helps define the character and temperament of those in the Northeast. While most of our snow is generated by regional storms moving through, Lake Champlain does influence the amount that falls in our basin.

Major snowstorms in the region tend to follow one of three tracks. The famous nor'easters consist of low-pressure systems clinging to the Atlantic coast. Winds flow in a counterclockwise direction into the center of the low-pressure area. Since we are west of the storm centers, our winds come from the north and east, giving the storms their name. This weather pattern accounts for about 30 percent of storms in the northern portion of the basin and perhaps more in the southern portion, closer to the ocean. Another 30 percent of major winter weather events originate as low-pressure systems in the eastern Canadian Rockies. These "Alberta clippers" tend to be smaller than nor'easters. Though occasionally producing large storms, this track generates many of the snows of six inches or less. The remaining 40 percent of storms track eastward through the Ohio and Mohawk River valleys. These are the storms that add to our snow totals while staying south of us.

Apart from the major snowstorms, Lake Champlain can cause local lake-effect snows. By definition, lake-effect snows occur only under conditions where no snow would be generated in the absence of the lake. One such storm dumped thirteen inches of snow in Cornwall, Vermont, in November 1996. Though lake-effect snows have caused some of the most infamous weather events around the Great Lakes (for instance seven feet of snow over eight days in Buffalo in 2001), they only rarely slam the Champlain Valley.

Three conditions must be met for lake-effect storms to form. First, a cold air mass must move over warmer water. Second, the temperature difference between the air in the upper atmosphere and water must be fairly high. (Upper atmosphere here is defined as the level at which air pressure equals 850 millibars; in a study of eight incidences of Lake Champlain–induced snow, the upper atmosphere ranged between 2,000 feet and 16,000 feet.) The temperature differential for the 1996 Cornwall storm was 75 degrees Fahrenheit, and 59 degrees is thought to be a minimum. Third, the two air masses must stay in contact long enough for the air to absorb moisture. The amount of time the two air masses stay in contact is determined by wind speed, wind direction, and the width of the water body. If wind speed is too high, then the upper cold-air layer moves through without having enough time to absorb water. Wind direction and water body width serve as limiting factors for lake-effect snows on Lake Champlain.

Since Lake Champlain is oblong, 120 miles long but at most 12 miles wide, only winds coming from near due north stay in contact with the water long enough to generate significant lake-effect snow. The distance that wind can blow across a water body (or other geographic feature) without being interrupted is known as its fetch, and the west-east fetch between Port Kent, New York, and Burlington, the longest on the lake, or Plattsburgh and Grand Isle, is too short for weather from the west to generate snow. If lake-effect snow does develop, it is most likely to strike Addison County, Vermont. That is where a wind blowing from the Richelieu River toward the Otter Creek hits land.

Lake Champlain can cause local lake-effect snow. (photo by Carolyn L. Bates)

Lake-effect snow is often most intense right near the shore. Once warm moist air hits land, it slows down because the friction of land is greater than that of water. However, there is still more wind coming from behind, and all the air has to go somewhere. It begins to rise into the cooler atmospheric layer above. Water in the air condenses, forming snow.

In addition to pure lake-effect snow, there are also more frequent lake-enhanced events. These occur when already existing storms become more severe in localized areas owing to the influence of the lake. At times, lake-enhanced snow can cause whiteouts when only minor flurries had been predicted.

As winter progresses, lake-effect snows become less likely. For one thing, as more of the lake becomes frozen, there is less opportunity for the air masses moving over it to absorb water. More important, as the temperature of the lake drops, it becomes improbable that a sufficient temperature differential between air and water will occur. When such a differential does occur, the upper air is usually too cold to hold much water.

For some, Lake Champlain's potential to add to snow accumulation in our winter wonderland means more days on the slopes. Others see it as one more reason to head south. Overall, it is just another aspect of the seasons on the lake.

○ The General

A series of depressions lies deep beneath Lake Champlain's surface, making the bottom vaguely reminiscent of a lunar landscape. The largest field of these pockmarks covers about 500 acres of Cumberland Bay, and they have an average diameter of 60 feet. The largest individual pockmark is in Burlington Bay and nicknamed "the General." It is over 132 feet in diameter and 13 feet in depth. How these pockmarks came to exist and what impact they have on the lake have been the subjects of research led by Pat and Tom Manley of Middlebury College.

In marine settings pockmarks are a common feature; but only as bottom surveys of lakes become more widespread have extensive fields been found in freshwater settings. Research into Lake Champlain's pockmarks was driven by an eight-year-long bottom survey completed in 2005. In addition to providing information about geologic features in Lake Champlain, the survey also resulted in the discovery of numerous shipwrecks.

A number of hypotheses exist about how pockmarks form. Some believe they are remnants of ancient meteor impacts. Others suggest that humans or even fish created them. The most widely accepted explanation is that they form when gas is released from below the surface. It is not uncommon, especially in marine settings, for gas to become trapped beneath an impermeable sediment layer. Pressure builds until the gas bursts forth, leaving a depression in its wake. However, this explanation does not seem plausible for Lake Champlain, because there are few areas of sufficient gas seepage into the lake.

The Manleys believe that upwelling groundwater caused Champlain's pockmarks, and studied the General for three years to test their hypothesis. Generally, the role of groundwater in the lake is underestimated. Mountainous terrain and thin upland surface deposits of glacial till mean groundwater moves quickly through the system, while in the lowlands the impermeability of ancient lake deposits minimizes groundwater flows. Thus lake level affects groundwater more than the groundwater affects lake level. Additionally, the vast extent of the drainage basin means surface flows dwarf any impacts from groundwater. Nonetheless there are localized areas where groundwater adds to the lake.

A number of lines of evidence support the groundwater hypothesis. One would expect groundwater to vary less in temperature than the sun-warmed and wind-cooled lake water, and indeed at one particular place near the edge of the pockmark the temperature is more uniform throughout the year. Additionally, underwater photographs have shown episodic suspension of sediments that could be explained by groundwater upwelling, although underwater currents are likely to be involved as well. Perhaps most convincing, the water in the pockmark has a higher mineral content, especially calcium and magnesium, than water outside the crater. Since the groundwater would have to pass through bedrock high in calcium and magnesium before reaching the pockmark, such evidence fits neatly with the hypothesis.

The excess calcium has led Mary Watzin of the University of Vermont to ask what effect pockmarks might have on the zebra mussels in the area and whether the mussels might be able to provide additional evidence for groundwater flows. The chemical composition of the mussels' bodies would reflect any changes in water chemistry over the period of time they were observed. Just as humans need calcium for strong bones and teeth, zebra mussels need it for thick shells. In recent years zebra mussel populations appear to have stabilized in the lake, and younger mussels tend to have thinner shells. The current hypothesis is that there isn't enough calcium in Lake Champlain's water to support more zebra mussels. If the pockmarks provide extra calcium, does that mean more, healthier zebra mussels hang out there?

Watzin placed caged mussels inside and outside the General and measured differences in their size and shell thickness after a growing season. She found that the mussels inside the pockmark did indeed have thicker shells, but they grew less in length than those outside. Although they had more calcium, there was actually less food available inside the pockmark. Zebra mussels filter food from the water column, and groundwater should have less food than lake water, but was there really too little lake water in the pockmark to feed the mussels? Groundwater flows from the pockmark were either too sporadic or too weak to be measured, so this explanation seemed incomplete.

Perhaps the phenomenon of stunted mussels was related to two other interesting observations. First, the Manleys had noted larger, coarser sediments inside the crater compared to outside. Second, there were no recent accumulations of sediment in the center of the General, only outside. If ground water upwelling was the only force acting on the pockmark, then newly accumulated sediments should be distributed evenly between the inside and outside.

The water column above the General is dynamic rather than stagnant. The internal seiche passes through the area approximately every four to five days during the summer. As the water column moves over the thirteen-foot-deep depression of the pockmark, it has to stretch to fill the extra space. When that happens, a little cyclone-like current develops, very similar to the dust devils one might see on windy days. Such a current could pick up fine sediments and zebra mussel food, then transport them out of the pockmark. If the groundwater upwelling was strong enough to suspend sediments, it would accentuate this process. Eventually, the only sediments left inside would be the large pieces that originally settled when the pockmark formed.

Evidence that pockmarks represent an influx of groundwater to the lake seems strong and getting stronger. Recently the Manleys used a new tool that allows them to look beneath the sediments at the bottom of the lake for potential gas deposits. Had such deposits been found under the pockmark, they would have undermined the groundwater hypothesis, but none were.

What such an influx means for water quality in the lake is less clear. Like most good research, work on the General has led to more questions than answers.

4

LIVING LAKE: PLANTS

Plants and algae provide the basis for life in the lake, yet they are regularly maligned as weeds or scum. Certainly in excess they prohibit enjoyment, but even then a certain degree of understanding can deepen appreciation of their role in the system. They form the base of the food chain, they provide hiding places for fish and other organisms in the lake, and many possess a hidden beauty, revealed only to the closest observers.

○ Where Land Meets Water

The transition from land to water can take many forms. Sometimes aquatic vegetation covers an area so thickly it is barely possible to tell where land ends and water begins. Sometimes a sandy shoreline provides little support for growing plants, and the delineation is stark. In still other areas the land abruptly disappears, plunging into the water where cliffs of limestone tower over the lake.

Delta

River deltas provide a gradual transition zone between basin and lake. The Missisquoi River has created the largest delta on Lake Champlain. As one moves downstream toward the mouth of the river at Missisquoi Bay, the graceful silver maples standing sentinel atop the high, levee-like banks give way to waves of grasslike rushes, as if the land were sinking into the water. In actuality, these grasslike plains hint at the slow accretion of new lands destined one day to host more silver maples.

The Missisquoi River is ninety-six miles long and carries thirty-five billion cubic yards of water each year, making it the second-largest river in the Champlain basin. With such a large drainage area, the Missisquoi River carries phenomenal amounts of sediment, much of which never leaves the delta. Each year the river floods during spring and with other heavy rains. When floodwaters hit the flatlands of the delta they fan out, spill over the banks, and deposit new sediments. The heaviest sediments pile up along the banks, creating high levees. Water becomes trapped outside these levees, giving rise to marshy areas loved by ducks and spawning pike. At least some of the river's nutrient pollution becomes permanently trapped behind these levees and in flooded forests.

Over thousands of years the dropped sediments have accumulated, creating a massive marshy area between the river's mouth and the bay's outlet. A vertical cross-section of the delta would look like a doorstop, with the thin end upstream, near Swanton, Vermont, and the thick end the loosely aggregated mucks at the mouth of the river.

At various times in the past the river would have drained more westerly or even to the south, bypassing Missisquoi Bay entirely (though to some degree bedrock limits how much the river can drain in other directions). An aerial view of the delta reveals what looks like a giant bird's footprint, with each "toe" representing an old abandoned channel.

The delta is a dynamic place. Some sediment accumulates in the main channel, choking the river and causing it to spill into the surrounding marshes. Since the landscape is so flat, the river cuts through the levees fairly easily when choking occurs, so new channels form. Channel switching occurs about every 150 to 300 years and is happening now. Much of the river's water actually exits via Dead Creek (which faces northeast, thus increasing the distance between the outlet of the river and the outlet of the bay) rather than by the "main stem."

Conditions that create deltas are not unique to the Missisquoi. Anywhere two water bodies merge and the incoming water

Missisquoi River delta (photo by Carolyn L. Bates)

is faster than the water being entered, a delta can form. To create a large, complex delta like that of the Missisquoi requires lots of water entering, a substantial slowing due to flat topography, and time. Other impressive deltas around the lake are at the mouths of the Ausable River, the Winooski River, and the Lamoille River.

Beach

Sand and waves, suntan lotion, bathing suits, a child's plastic pail and shovel for building castles: spending a day at the beach is a long-standing summer tradition. So why do beaches form along some coves on Lake Champlain but not others?

Most of Lake Champlain's beaches have two things in common: they are north of outlets to large rivers, and they face south. Rivers feed beaches by supplying sand. The reason sand is deposited along the lakeshore is similar to the reasons it is deposited in deltas, and has to do with the energy and speed of the moving water. Imagine running down a street when suddenly the road

Beach near Appletree Point (photo by Carolyn L. Bates)

in front of you is blocked by pedestrians; you would be forced to slow down and weave around people. As rivers enter Lake Champlain they, too, slow down as their running water merges with the mass of comparatively still water in the lake. As moving water slows it loses energy and thus its ability to carry sediment. Sensibly it drops the heaviest sediment first—sand. Other particles, silt and clay, are carried farther out into the open lake.

So why are the beaches north of river outlets and facing south? Back to the running analogy: imagine that the crowd of pedestrians is moving in one direction. Once you have entered the crowd, it would take much more work to move in a direction against their flow. Currents in Lake Champlain generally flow north, toward the lake's outlet to the Richelieu River. As river water enters the lake it, too, flows north, joining the lake's current. If there is a suitable expanse of relatively flat land facing south, winds and the current push sand onto that land, forming a beach.

A few Lake Champlain beaches have also developed in bays between two peninsulas. In these situations, the peninsulas bear the full force of waves pounding against them. Eroded sand from the peninsulas then washes into the bays and is pushed toward shore. Examples of this type of beach can be found at Point Au Roche State Park in New York and at the head of Kingsland Bay in Vermont.

Under natural conditions, the dunes on beaches change seasonally. During the summer, low lake levels expose an expanse of sand between the dunes and the water, called the back shore. This is where you set up your blankets when visiting the beach. Hot weather dries the sand, which wind then picks up and redeposits on the dunes farther inland. During the winter the inland migration of sand reverses. High-energy winter and spring storms, coupled with higher lake levels, send waves crashing against the beach and the closest dunes. Each wave scoops up some sand and drags it into the lake. Since sand is heavy, it usually does not go far; rather it replenishes the back shore and forms a sandbar a short distance out from the beach. Sandbars help dissipate the energy of storms by causing waves to break farther from shore. The cycle of being torn down in the winter and rebuilt in the summer makes sand dunes dynamic places.

Dunes move not only on a seasonal time scale, but on a geologic time scale as well. As lake levels rise or fall due to the effects of glaciers or global warming, the beaches move inland or toward the water. There is evidence that lake levels have been rising over the past few thousand years. Among the dunes at Plattsburgh Municipal Beach you can find old stumps, indicating that the area now occupied by the dunes was once part of a forest. Beneath the dunes in Alburg, Vermont, lies a layer of peat, decayed moss, indicating that the area the dunes now occupy once sported a very different ground covering, perhaps a wetland or conifer forest.

Sand dunes are a harsh environment where few plants can make a living. Since sand particles are relatively large (compared to clay), water runs through the dunes quickly, leaving little in storage for dry times. The absence of water also causes sand's surface temperature to fluctuate wildly within a day. Imagine walking over sand in bare feet on a typical summer day at two o'clock in the afternoon compared to eight in the morning. Finally, sand offers few of the essential nutrients plants need. The roots of plants that do survive, particularly beach grasses, hold the dunes together against the onslaught of winter waves by knitting a matrix below the surface of the dunes to which sand particles cling.

There are three plant species in the Champlain basin found only on beaches: American beach grass, beach pea, and beach heather. Though these plants can be prolific on the sands of beaches and dunes, their habitat is very restricted. They are known from only six beaches around the lake, and no beach contains all three. Since populations of these plants are more common along the oceans, according to Dr. Sonja Schmitz, a student of beaches and beach plants, our populations are relics of a time when Lake Champlain was a saltwater sea. Then, seeds could have traveled via a saltwater corridor through the St. Lawrence and Richelieu rivers to the shores of Lake Champlain. Schmitz's research has shown that the strains of American beach grass and beach pea on the shores of Lake Champlain are genetically distinct from their maritime cousins. The American beach grass will flower up to two months earlier than comparable populations along the Atlantic, suggesting it may be a distinct species.

The greatest threat to beach dunes and dune-adapted plants is the development of houses and camps along shorelines. Sandy soils drain well, so septic systems are easy to install. Incrementally, houses and developments have popped up on beaches throughout the Champlain basin, leaving only a few examples of natural beaches for the public and for the plants.

Cedar Bluffs

A common motif in comic books presents characters as having two distinct personalities. Think of mild-mannered Clark Kent and the high-flying Superman, or inept Peter Parker and the amazing Spider-Man. Such dual personalities can be found in the natural world as well, and one of the more common examples regularly occurs on the shores of Lake Champlain.

White cedar trees (*Thuja occidentalis*, or eastern arborvitae) dominate in very wet or very dry conditions, but seldom in between. Typically, white cedars thrive in lowland swamps or along the banks of rivers. However, around Lake Champlain they are frequently found atop shoreline cliffs. Here shallow soils and incessant winds create a dry setting where the trees form a thick, dark forest. Within several hundred feet of the cliff top, the cedars typically give way to other upland community types like hardwood forests.

White cedar on shoreline cliff at Burton Island (photo by Jeanne Stark)

There are commonalities between the two very different environments—rich soils and stressful growing conditions. Cliffs hosting white cedars are invariably composed of limestone or dolomite, two calcium-based rocks. Cedar-dominated wetlands also occur in association with calcium-rich bedrock. Just as growing bodies use the calcium in milk for strong bones and teeth, and zebra mussels use calcium to harden their shells, plants use calcium to strengthen cell walls. Plant communities growing on limestone-derived soils frequently contain species unusual in more calcium-poor areas. Dolomite adds magnesium as well as calcium. Stressful growing conditions reduce competition from faster-growing species like white pine. Along the cliffs, stress comes from wind, shallow soil, and limited water. In the swamps, stress comes from the constant inundation of roots, which limits oxygen supply. Harsh conditions, coupled with numerous cavities created by woodpeckers and fallen limbs, produce twisted and deformed trees. Many topple in strong storms, strewn about like matchsticks.

It is unwise to guess the age of a tree from its size, and white cedars demonstrate why. They can attain great age without achieving great stature. In their guide to the natural communities of Vermont, naturalists Elizabeth Thompson and Eric Sorenson describe cedar trees over 300 years old. Some cliff-top trees with hollow trunks are over 200 years old yet less than fifteen feet tall. In similar communities around Lake Ontario, 1,000-year-old cedars have been documented. Meanwhile, white pines growing in association with the cedars can tower above them despite being much younger.

Cedar communities evoke calm excitement in me, a contradiction befitting the dual nature of the trees themselves. The gorgeous vegetation, which offers protection from the heat of summer or the winds and snows of winter, elicits a sense of calm. The excitement emanates from the unknown treasures that might be concealed by the thick branches—perhaps a tiny saw-whet owl watching from a woodpecker cavity, a whip-poor-will perched on a tree limb, or a ram's head lady slipper hiding among the patches of sedge on the forest floor. Yellow-rumped warblers flit around in the branches, and the broken and jumbled rocks of the forest floor provide cover for squirrels and chipmunks.

Occasionally the thick trees satisfy my anticipation. One December I found myself in a cedar swamp near dusk. It was the end of a Christmas Bird Count, and I had walked into the area hoping to add a red-breasted nuthatch or golden-crowned kinglet to my day's list. The woods were quiet, and I was tired, so I attempted to call the birds to me by squeaking and pishing. Instead of the tiny songbirds, a beautiful barred owl silently drifted to within about ten feet, perhaps mistaking my squeaks for a distressed mouse. The bird landed on a nearby branch about seven feet off the ground, framed by green boughs and bits of hanging snow. It took one look at me and just as silently disappeared back into the woods.

The proximity of cedar communities to the lake and the views offered from the cliff tops make this habitat type highly attractive to developers. Nonetheless, Lake Champlain is fortunate to host an abundance of protected, readily accessible examples of cedar bluffs. In New York they can be found on Valcour Island and Split Rock Mountain, both parts of the Adirondack Park. In Vermont, a number of state parks, including Kingsland Bay, Niquette Bay, and Highgate, host the trees.

○ Falling Leaves: Investing in the Food Chain

Rivers entering Lake Champlain carry more than the sediment that builds deltas or beaches; they also carry food for the creatures that live in the lake. Throughout the summer, trees invest in short-term, high-yield leaves to collect sunlight, and then place the dividends in long-term wood. As autumn's panoply of colors blankets the mountains of the Champlain Valley, the trees begin dumping their investment like Enron executives before an inevitable downturn. If they tried to hold on to their leaves, winter's snow and winds would be more likely to pull down good wood. Many of those leaves end up in headwater streams of Lake Champlain, where they represent the primary energy input for the river system.

In most ecosystems, energy comes directly from the sun, but that resource is less available for small streams. At their starting points streams are narrow, and during the growing season limbs arc out from the banks. Leaves on these branches intercept sunlight and extract its energy before it can reach the water. Without sunlight there can be no growth of plants or algae in the water. Since plants usually form the base of any food chain, their absence represents a limitation. Instead the food chain depends upon whatever falls into the water.

As an energy source, fallen leaves are like the stocks of bankrupt companies: they have the same general appearance as leaves on trees but much less value. Once they are in the water, only bacteria and fungi are suited to take advantage of them as an energy source. In the process of feeding upon leaves, bacteria and fungi transform the carbon-based compounds (the energy source) into sugars more usable to other organisms, while at the same time getting some of their necessary daily servings of minerals directly from the water column. Thus they concentrate minerals for organisms above them on the food chain.

Because of their ability to concentrate energy and nutrients even without sunlight, bacteria and fungi serve as the base of this relatively nutrient-poor food chain. Mayflies graze them from leaves much as we might scrape the filling off an Oreo cookie. Caddis flies spin webs that they sweep through the water to collect bits and pieces of detritus with attached bacteria. They then pull their nets into self-constructed rock hideaways where they can eat in peace. Thus, slowly, what little value was left in those discarded leaves is further concentrated.

The ability of organisms to accumulate nutrients is enhanced by an abundance of oxygen in headwater streams. There are two reasons oxygen is so prevalent in the upper reaches of streams. First, headwaters tend to have a steeper slope with more rocks, and water leaping and cascading over rocks incorporates oxygen from the air. Second, and most important, headwaters are colder because arcing branches intercept sunlight, shading and cooling the water. Cooler water can hold more gases—like oxygen—than warm water can. That is why a soda left in the sun will go flat much more quickly than one in the refrigerator.

While in general nature recycles its riches—leaf to soil to leaf again—those leaves that enter the river begin a one-way journey out of the system and toward Lake Champlain. Along the way the river accumulates more and more nutrient wealth, from both natural and artificial sources. Natural sources include trees and animals. Additionally, once the river becomes broad enough that trees no longer shade its entire width, the availability of sunlight increases, allowing plants to use those nutrients more effectively. The added algae and plant growth supplements bacteria at the base of the food chain.

Changes in the river's shape that allow algae to thrive also result in less available oxygen. The absence of shade leads to an increase in water temperature, and the wider river has fewer cascades and ripples. Creatures seeking to make use of the excess nutrients must either be more sedentary to reduce their need for oxygen, or mobile enough to escape periods of temporary oxygen depletion. Some insects in slow-moving reaches rely on atmospheric oxygen rather than what is dissolved in the water.

Back upstream, there are few opportunities for resources to be redistributed. Some fish move upstream to spawn and then die, representing one route of material transfer. Also, many aquatic insects hatch and become flying terrestrial adults that instinctively head upstream to deposit their eggs.

Spring floods accelerate the transfer of wealth downstream by eroding stream banks, while at the same time providing lateral movement from the river to the land. The energy of floods transports large slugs of sediment and debris toward the lake. However, some of the debris remains on land, where it can be sequestered in soil or vegetation.

Once water reaches Lake Champlain it enters yet another ecological zone. Sunlight touches the lake across the length and breadth of its surface. Every portion of the surface is a potential incubator, but the necessary nutrients for growth are distributed unevenly. Some rivers carry more and some less, but those that carry more are diluted once they mix with those that carry less. Segments of the lake with large volumes of water, like the Main Lake, provide better dilution than do areas with less volume, like Missisquoi Bay, thus in part explaining differences in plant productivity in these two systems.

Putting Away the Groceries: Food Storage in Lake Champlain

My wife and I have a disagreement about the organization of food in the kitchen. She has a system—a place for everything, and everything in its place. My sense of domestic order, on the other hand, is substantially less refined. What difference does it make whether you put the cereal in the cupboard over the sink or in the pantry? Either way it ends up in someone's belly. For years, scientists' thoughts about plant food in Lake Champlain were akin to my kitchen filing strategy: it did not really matter where it goes, once it is in the water. There is growing evidence, however, that such distinctions do matter.

A long-term management goal for Lake Champlain has been to limit plant food, principally phosphorus, from entering the lake, in an effort to control nuisance algae blooms. (Opportunities for nutrients to *leave* the lake are limited; in essence, the only exits are the Richelieu River and fish taken out by humans and other predators.) To that end, sewage treatment plants have been upgraded; many farming practices have been modified to better control nutrients in manure; and some buffer zones along some streams have been protected.

However, once the food enters the lake, it doesn't necessarily all go into algae. There are a limited number of other compartments in which it can be stored, most notably fish, zooplankton, sediment, and, in shallow sections, emergent plants. It is in the shallow parts of the lake that the issue of where food gets stored becomes most important.

Nutrient-rich shallow lakes (or lake segments) tend to be dominated either by emergent plants (also known as weeds) or by algae blooms, depending on how clear the water is. If the water is clear, light penetrates to the bottom, and emergent plants make their way to the surface. If the water is murky, algae take advantage of the excess nutrients instead. As nutrient concentrations increase, lakes are more likely to be dominated by algae.

Lakes can switch from algae dominance to weed dominance, but it's not easy to do so. Managers of Big Muskego Lake in Wisconsin were able to shift nutrient storage in their lake's biota from algae to a wide diversity of emergent plants through a three-step process. First, they drew down the water for over a year. This killed carp that stir up bottom sediments and make water murky, preventing the growth of many emergent marsh plants. The death of the emergent plants removes hiding places for other fish and plankton that provide food for those fish. Second, they restocked the lake with a diverse assemblage of fish, including lots of pike and walleye. By including a high density of predators, they increased pressure on fish that eat zooplankton. Thus more zooplankton were available to eat algae. Finally, they severely limited the size and number of fish that could be removed by anglers so that the stocked fish could better survive and continue to control smaller fish.

Lake Zwemlust in Denmark was shifted in the other direction. There extensive emergent vegetation interfered with swimming, so herbicides were applied. However, since the nutrients fueling plant growth were still present, the lake was soon covered with blooms of blue-green algae instead. More recently managers of Lake Zwemlust have been able to bring back the weeds, utilizing a strategy similar to the one at Big Muskego.

The amount of food stored in sediments can have huge implications as well. As one example, great strides have been made in controlling phosphorus inputs to St. Albans Bay by upgrading the sewage treatment plant and investing heavily in reducing pollution from farms. However, nutrient concentrations in the water column still exceed accepted standards. Unfortunately, years of excess phosphorus were saved in the bay's sediments, like piles of canned goods in a bomb cellar from the 1950s. Whenever concentrations in the water column start to get low, a new can is opened. No one can say for sure how many cans are still down there.

The lessons from Big Muskego and Zwemlust don't apply to the whole of Lake Champlain; emergent plants can't grow in deep portions of the lake, for example. Additionally, the presence of murk-tolerant Eurasian water milfoil and water-clarifying zebra mussels complicates the dynamics. However, those lessons force recognition of the limits of management in shallow lake segments like St. Albans and Missisquoi bays. Here lake users cannot expect simultaneous elimination of both algae blooms and emergent plants. Once the extra groceries get into those particular cabinets, they end up in some sort of unwanted plant growth.

○ Water Plants

Many myths and folktales tell of semihuman creatures living aquatic lives, like the half-fish mermaids or gill-breathing Atlanteans. Though people have not actually evolved underwater forms, many plants have. Flowering plants first evolved on land, suggesting that aquatic flowering species derived from the original terrestrial types. The transition likely occurred many times, though there are still substantially fewer species that live in the water.

Just as mermaids and Atlanteans needed special adaptations for life underwater, so do plants. The limited light available for food production constitutes the principal challenge. When light strikes water, a portion is reflected back to the atmosphere. Another portion strikes particles in the water and bounces around. Therefore, less is available for photosynthesis. Aquatic plants have adapted by increasing their efficiency at low light levels, but still there are very few species that can grow below twenty-six feet in depth.

Exchange of oxygen and carbon dioxide can also be more challenging for water plants. Water holds less of each gas than air. During the day, carbon dioxide levels in the water drop while plants use it to make food. Meanwhile, oxygen, a by-product of food production, increases. At night the relative concentrations reverse. Many aquatic plants have large spaces between their cells where oxygen can be stored to fuel cell functions, but such storage tends to be very short-term.

Adaptations to facilitate the capture of light and exchange of gases are visible in the leaves of aquatic plants. Aquatic plants produce three general types of leaves: aerial, floating, or submerged. Aerial leaves, as seen in cattails and sedges, avoid all the problems of underwater living by not being underwater. The only real adaptation needed is sufficient food storage in the seed for the stem or leaf to grow through the water column. These leaves greatly increase the humidity of marshy areas on hot summer days by moving large amounts of water into the atmosphere. Floating leaves such as those of water chestnut or duckweed capture light before it has a chance to diffuse underwater, but unlike terrestrial leaves or even underwater leaves they can move only in two rather than three dimensions. Thus it is more difficult to adjust to changes in light availability caused by shading from above. As a result, floating leaves tend to spread apart rather than overlap one another, as might happen with tree leaves. Floating leaves are roughly circular in shape, with a tough leathery texture that prevents wind and waves from tearing them. They concentrate their cells for gas exchange at the top of the leaf, while the bottom contains large air spaces that offer buoyancy. Submerged leaves provide large surface areas relative to the interior area, which increases the area over which gas exchange can occur. They can be deeply divided or feathery in appearance. Eurasian water milfoil, whose Latin genus name, *Myriophyllum*, translates as "countless leaves," is one example. Alternatively, submerged leaves may be very long and thin, like eelgrass (also known as wild celery). Submerged leaves are pliable, taking advantage of the water column itself for support rather than the rigid internal architecture needed by aerial leaves.

On land, plants have developed elaborate mechanisms to ensure pollen passes from male flowers to female flowers through wind or intermediate pollinators, thus ensuring reproduction. Water presents a different challenge. Pollen cannot move through water as it can through air, and the reliable insect pollinators are much less abundant. Most aquatic plants compensate by holding their flowers above the surface of the water. Once pollination has been completed, the stem holding the flower might coil, as in water lilies, pulling the flower down below the water surface and out of sight from seed and fruit predators. A few plants actually pass pollen through the water. One such species is coontail, a common native underwater plant sometimes mistaken for Eurasian water milfoil. In this species, male flowers break off the plant and float to the surface. Once there, they drop pollen, which sinks down onto the female flowers, which remain below. Asexual, vegetative growth from existing plant material is still the most common form of reproduction, despite the many fascinating strategies that some species have developed.

In some versions of legends, aquatic people lose their fish halves and are able to walk on land. Similarly, some aquatic plants can develop a land form that is quite different from their aquatic stage. This allows them to survive periods of low water levels.

Though most people think of underwater plants as invasive weeds, the majority of Lake Champlain's nearly one hundred species are actually native and play important roles in the lake's ecosystem. By their mere existence, underwater plants increase the available habitat for other organisms. They provide hiding places, a substrate to move or grow upon, and a food source for everything from other plants to snails to microscopic creatures to fish. Aquatic plants such as eelgrass and cattails provide food for ducks and other wildlife.

In very high densities, aquatic plants can also make life difficult for other organisms by depleting the amount of oxygen available in the water column. Oxygen depletion is most common at night, on cloudy days, or when the plants form a continuous surface cover. Under these conditions photosynthesis slows, meaning oxygen is still used by the plants but is not returned to water. Oxygen can also be depleted when large amounts of plant material die either at the end of a growing season or due to continual shedding of leaves. The dead material leads to a boom in oxygen-hungry decomposers.

Blue-green Algae: What's the Risk?

The ability of freshwater algae to produce toxins has been recognized since at least 1838, when a "bloom"—an extensive surface growth—in Australia led to the deaths of numerous livestock. Anecdotal evidence exists of illness caused by swimming in or drinking from algae-filled waters, but prior reports did not draw a direct link between algae and health effects. In the last twenty years, incidents of animal poisonings attributed to algae blooms have been recorded in Argentina, Australia, Canada, Finland, Norway, England, Scotland, and on Lake Champlain.

In recent years, reports of human illness associated with algae outbreaks have led to increased attention and research into this phenomenon. Most illnesses are limited to upset stomachs, diarrhea, vomiting, or skin irritations. The most serious impact from algae occurred in 1996 in Brazil, when toxins got into dialysis machines, and more than fifty patients died. Other than that incident, only one human death has been attributed to poisoning from algae, and the particulars of that case leave room for doubt as

Eelgrass and cattails provide food for ducks and other wildlife. (photo by Carolyn L. Bates)

to the exact cause of death. Compare this to an average of nine drowning incidents per day in the United States, according to 2000 data from the U.S. Center for Disease Control.

In fresh water, toxic blooms are produced by blue-green algae—plantlike bacteria that form a natural component of any lake ecosystem. (Blue-green algae are also called cyanobacteria.) Like plants, they can use the energy of the sun to fuel their metabolic processes and grow. However, their cells lack internal structures, organelles, that define plants and other "higher" organisms. Therefore blue-greens are considered bacteria.

Excess nutrient concentrations facilitate growth of any algae. Phosphorus is the nutrient whose absence apparently limits most algae growth. Nitrogen is important as well, but many blue-greens, unlike other algae, are able to use available nitrogen from the air. The exact triggers of bloom formation are not known. Algae undergo predictable seasonal changes in dominance, with blue-greens being most prevalent later in the summer, in part due to the ability of some to capture nitrogen at a time when rivers are bringing less of that nutrient to the lake.

Two categories of algae toxins have been identified at various times in Lake Champlain, and we have a good idea of the specific species that produce them. Mycrocystin acts on the liver and is produced by species in the genus *Microcystis*. Anatoxins act on the nervous system and are produced by species in the genera *Anabena* and *Aphanizomenon*.

We do not know when or how toxic species actually produce toxins, and differences often occur between water bodies. For example, Onondaga Lake, near Syracuse, New York, is regularly plagued by blue-green algae outbreaks of a species known to produce toxins. However, toxins are almost never found in the lake. On the other hand, nearby Oneida Lake has not been subject to extensive algae blooms, yet concentrations of toxins are relatively high. On Lake Champlain, in Missisquoi Bay the dominant blue-green algae is *Microcystis*. Outside Missisquoi Bay, blooms tend to be dominated by other genera. We do not know why.

We are also not really sure why algae produce toxins. Predator avoidance is the most logical hypothesis, and indeed it has been shown that zebra mussels reject toxic species while feeding on nontoxic species. However, there is some evidence that the chemicals we think of as toxins are used by the algae to sense the world around them. Alternatively, toxins may be used to inhibit competing algae more than to avoid predators.

Improvements in analytical techniques and increased attention to blue-green algae blooms have enhanced our ability to detect and react to toxins. As a result, scientists have found toxins in many more water bodies than previously expected. During the summer of 2007, blue-greens were detected in numerous Quebec water bodies for the first time, in a year when they were practically absent from Missisquoi Bay.

No one had even thought to look for toxic algae on Lake Champlain prior to 1999, when a bloom claimed the lives of three dogs. Monitoring for toxins began the following

Excess nutrient concentrations facilitate growth of algae. (photo by Ron Haskell)

summer and gradually grew to include more and more of the lake. Toxins may have been in the lake for decades or centuries prior to 1999 (though there is evidence of a shift in species dominance in the northern part of the lake), but we have only a few summers' worth of data to judge what a "normal" concentration is.

Since the phenomenon of toxic algae on Lake Champlain has only recently been recognized and is outside the immediate control of the public, perceptions of risk are enhanced. People are generally more worried about risks they just learned about than familiar ones. Think of the different public perceptions toward mad cow disease or West Nile virus, compared to the flu virus, which annually kills many more people. Situations beyond the control of individuals also tend to be perceived as riskier. Hence, people worry much more about flying, a fairly safe activity, than they do about driving, though auto accidents are the fifth-leading cause of death in the United States.

It is not entirely clear what level of toxins in the water constitutes a public health risk. As a result, different governmental agencies respond in different manners to the same situation. The World Health Organization (WHO) had determined that one microgram of toxins in a liter of water constituted a health risk, but that was based on long-term exposure through drinking water. If toxin concentrations reach this level, Canadian officials would close beaches indefinitely, Vermont officials would post temporary warnings, and New York officials might not do anything (this level has not been reported along the New York side of the lake). The various governments' different reactions have furthered confusion about risks associated with blue-green algae. Recently the WHO revised its standards for recreational exposure, determining that concentrations between two and ten micrograms per liter represented a "relatively low probability of adverse health effects."

Though the public tends to perceive toxic algae as riskier than they actually are, that does not mean there is no risk. Fortunately, steps can be taken to reduce risk. In short, avoid swimming or wading when the water looks disgusting. Toxin concentrations are highest where algae cell densities are highest, right in the thick scums that accumulate near shore. Toxin concentrations are also highest when the algae cells begin to break down and the toxins are released into the water. This, too, occurs near shore as algae are washed up and begin to decompose in the sun.

So, how dangerous are toxic algae? Compared to most risks people face every day, they rank pretty low. And when considering the threat posed by toxic algae to recreation on the lake, it is important to maintain perspective. Toxic algae are a worldwide phenomenon. Though our knowledge of them on Lake Champlain is new and growing, it is likely they have been here for a long time. Governments are still struggling to identify the best approach to public outreach about the risks, but when algae blooms do form, simply avoiding accumulations of green scum minimizes risk of illness.

○ Little Glass Houses

A world of eight-spoked stars, helically twisted place mats, and long wands filled with gobs of green jelly opened before my eyes when I first looked upon the diatoms, the group that dominates most of Lake Champlain's algae community. Although blue-green algae regularly make headlines, for most of the lake and most of the year the algal community is unremarkable in human terms. We do not see them, and they do not irritate us. Only when one looks through a microscope do the delicate shapes and forms of the diatoms appear.

During the Victorian era in England, microscopes were popular with the well-to-do, and diatoms were one of the favored subjects of study. Patient artists would even arrange the ornate cells in intricate patterns, creating works of art. Some of the resulting preserved slides are on display in museums today.

The elaborate shapes occur because diatoms live within "glass houses." Their cell walls are made of two plates of silica, the thinnest windows imaginable. Apparently the glass plates help them accumulate carbon dioxide and increase the efficiency of photosynthesis. The intricate shapes of the diatoms, so intriguing under the microscope, increase the surface area of the organisms, further enhancing carbon dioxide accumulation.

Classification of diatoms is based upon variations in the shape of their glass houses. Centric diatoms are rounded. The spherical shape makes them quite buoyant, and they are more common in marine environments than the second group, called pennate diatoms. These can be elongated or flattened, but they all have bilateral symmetry, which means only one imaginary line drawn through an individual can divide it into two nearly identical halves. Humans are also bilaterally symmetrical. Most freshwater diatoms, including all the ones described in the opening paragraph, are pennate (the eight-spoked star is actually a colony of eight different individuals).

In addition to their beauty, diatoms are thought to capture 20 to 25 percent of all the solar energy in the world used for living organisms. Of course, most of this capture takes place in the oceans. Diatoms' tremendous ability to convert sunlight to usable energy makes them critically important in the lake food web, as they provide sustenance for many of the zooplankton upon which fish feed.

Typically we think of green plants capturing sunlight. However, diatoms appear more yellow-brown, because they utilize accessory pigments in addition to the more typical green chlorophyll. These accessory pigments absorb light of longer wavelengths, hence the difference in color. Longer wavelengths offer less energy but penetrate farther into the water. So what the diatoms lose in efficiency, they regain by their ability to extend their range into deeper water.

Changes in diatom communities can be linked to changes in the ecological condition of the water body in which they live. Since the silica of diatoms accumulates, cores of lake-bottom sediments may show different species compositions over time. In this way, diatoms have been used to assess the extent of acidification of Adirondack lakes and to determine changes in the nutrient status of lakes throughout North America.

In Lake Champlain, as in most lakes, diatoms are abundant during the spring and early summer when excess silica from spring runoff promotes their growth. Silica becomes less available later in the summer. First the diatoms tie it up, and then it becomes trapped in organisms that eat diatoms or sinks to the bottom of the lake as diatoms die.

Since glass does not readily dissolve back into the water column, once diatoms settle to the bottom, the silica stays there, accumulating over millennia. Two commercially valuable products have resulted from ancient accumulations of diatoms. One, diatomaceous earth, is commonly used for filtration, as a polish, in paints to increase reflectivity, or as insulation. The other, resulting from even older deposits, is the oil that today fuels our cars and heats our homes.

Not all algae ruin a day at the beach. Beautiful, ecologically important, indicators of change, and economically valuable, these initially unremarkable glass houses can help offset some of the negative news about algae brought on by the blue-greens.

5

LIVING LAKE: ANIMALS

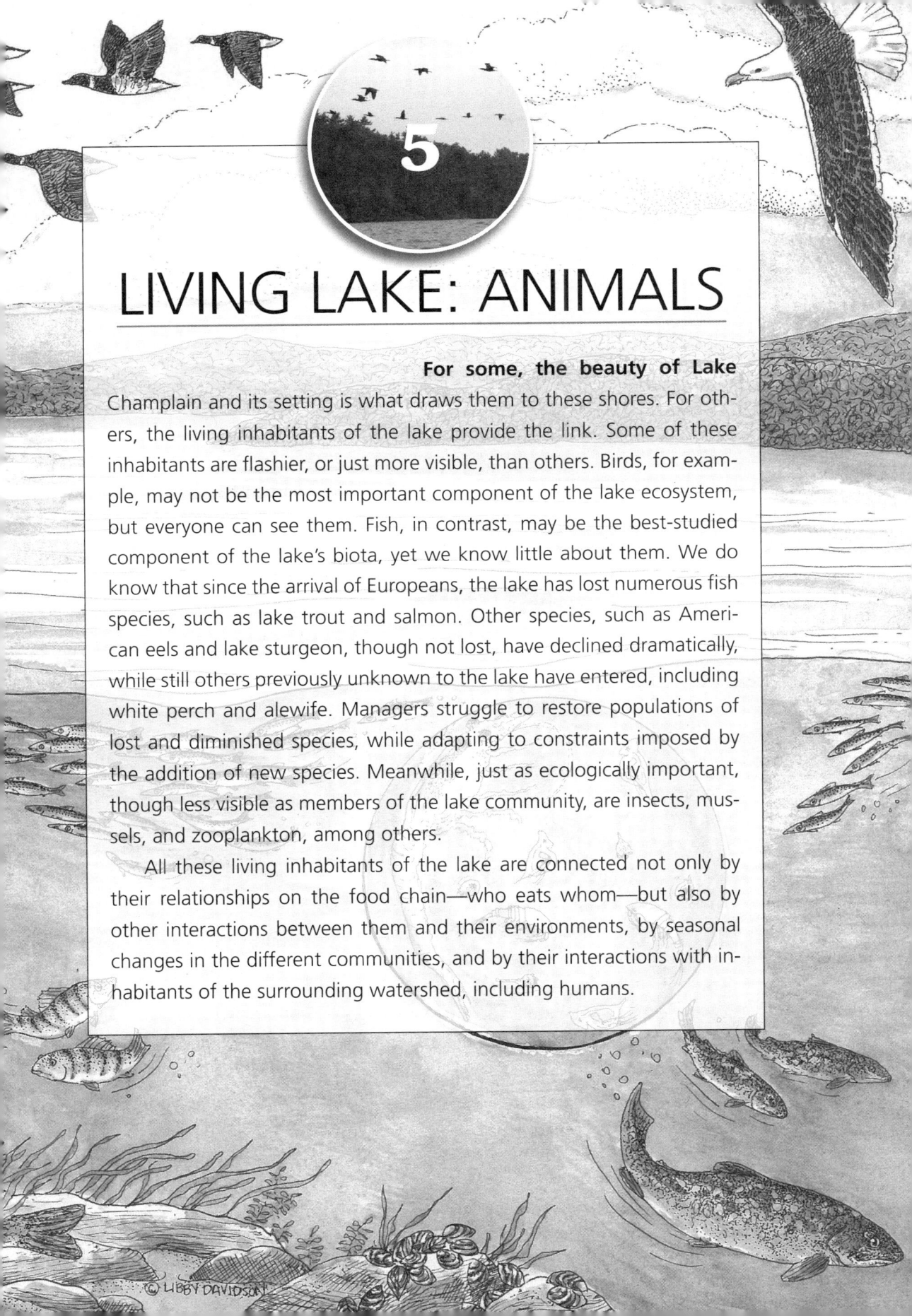

For some, the beauty of Lake Champlain and its setting is what draws them to these shores. For others, the living inhabitants of the lake provide the link. Some of these inhabitants are flashier, or just more visible, than others. Birds, for example, may not be the most important component of the lake ecosystem, but everyone can see them. Fish, in contrast, may be the best-studied component of the lake's biota, yet we know little about them. We do know that since the arrival of Europeans, the lake has lost numerous fish species, such as lake trout and salmon. Other species, such as American eels and lake sturgeon, though not lost, have declined dramatically, while still others previously unknown to the lake have entered, including white perch and alewife. Managers struggle to restore populations of lost and diminished species, while adapting to constraints imposed by the addition of new species. Meanwhile, just as ecologically important, though less visible as members of the lake community, are insects, mussels, and zooplankton, among others.

All these living inhabitants of the lake are connected not only by their relationships on the food chain—who eats whom—but also by other interactions between them and their environments, by seasonal changes in the different communities, and by their interactions with inhabitants of the surrounding watershed, including humans.

○ A Night for the Birds

The boat drifted quietly through the darkness to the cobble shore of the island as the calls of thousands of gulls rang through the air. The moon would not rise for another three or four hours, and we needed to finish our mission by then. The smell of fish and guano strengthened. We hopped out, moored the boat, and took up our arms. Adam laid out the assault plan: we would charge over the sandy ridge and through the thistle toward our first target group, just beyond the bushes. Adam Duerr was a doctoral candidate at the University of Vermont, and our arms were not guns, but large nets on seven-foot-long poles. Our quarry was double-crested cormorants.

We tried to step around the unflustered gulls and tussocks of grass as we approached the first nesting area. Our mission was to capture and band the adults, which were glossier than the nearly fledged young, as well as more likely to run away from us. As we reached the nest all was confusion; birds squawked and fluttered away, and my companions scattered in pursuit. With a headlamp providing the only light, I could not tell the glossy black birds from the dull black ones. I cued into their behavior, spied one racing awkwardly away, and clamped my net down over it.

Unfortunately, the bird I caught was a juvenile, and my success at catching adults did not improve much as the evening progressed. I netted only one, while our group of five caught twenty-nine birds. Once caught, each bird was carefully held until Duerr banded both legs and made various measurements of its legs, bill, wings, and tail feathers. The care was for our own sake as well as the cormorants'. The birds' long, sharp, powerful bills with serrated edges evolved for catching fish were quite capable of leaving a nasty cut in a finger or hand.

The birds' fish-catching ability has drawn a great deal of attention and irritation. Anglers sometimes see the adults successfully catching big fish, note the large and growing colonies, and wonder about the impact on the lake's fishery. Cormorants seem to catch whatever is available when and where they are hunting; they don't feed preferentially on any given fish species. On Lake Champlain they eat a large number of small perch, but no meaningful impacts on the population have been documented.

Double-crested cormorants have not always been common on Lake Champlain. The 1974 edition of *Birds of New York* describes their status inland as "rare to uncommon at any time" and cites Gull Island on Lake Ontario as the only known inland breeding site. According to the 1985 *Atlas of Breeding Birds of Vermont*, in 1982 "the first known breeding of the double-crested cormorant in Vermont occurred, in a stick nest in a dead tree near the water on Young Island [on the northwest side of Grand Isle]; while one bird incubated, 27 looked on. In 1983, the breeding colony had exploded to 34 nests on trees fringing the island and adults numbered 108."

Exploded indeed. The pesticide DDT once decimated the double-crested cormorant population, but its phase-out and an increase in winter food supply in the South (due to fish farms and new reservoirs) have led to skyrocketing growth. The cormorant population on Lake Champlain grew more than 20 percent per year through the mid-'90s, peaking at over 20,000 birds by 1999, in a trend similar to what occurred through much of the Northeast. However, the lake's cormorant population fell after 1999 and as of 2006 was still below 1999 levels.

Cormorants are messy nesters. The copious guano they produce acidifies soil around their nests, making it difficult for vegetation to grow. They tear twigs off nest trees, further accelerating the denuding of islands. On the largest of the Four Brothers, a group of islands between Shelburne and Willsboro, the once healthy pine forest has been reduced to a skeleton of its former self. Though cormorants may prefer a paucity of vegetation, other colonial nesting birds such as black-crowned night herons, great blue herons, and cattle egrets do not, and they may abandon their rookeries after cormorants arrive.

The Vermont Fish & Wildlife Department took action to limit cormorants' nesting success on Lake Champlain beginning in 1994. Initial efforts were focused on preventing cormorants from establishing colonies on Mud and Poppasquash islands. Starting in 1999 the department received permits from the U.S. Fish and Wildlife Service to expand those efforts and apply corn oil to eggs, most of which were on Young Island, but some were on other smaller islands as well. The oil prevented eggs from developing and hatching.

However, control actions have unforeseen consequences, as revealed by Duerr's work. In addition to the birds banded on the Four Brothers islands, where no cormorant control occurred, he also banded birds on Young Island, where cormorant nests were oiled. That way he could compare how often birds from the two populations changed islands.

He found that any decreases in cormorant nests on Young Island caused by oiling were offset by increases in nesting in other locations, especially Four Brothers, but also at the Missisquoi National Wildlife Refuge, at Crown Point, and on other small islands. Cormorants were also reportedly more numerous along the St. Lawrence River in Quebec Province following egg oiling on Lake Champlain. The cormorants had simply moved.

The shift southward of the Lake Champlain population from Young Island to the Four Brothers also affected the diet of the birds. Instead of foraging in the north, the birds on Four Brothers spent more time in the central part of the lake, and they ate more. It had been easier for the birds to fill themselves from the fishing grounds in the north; when they were around Four Brothers they used more energy gathering food and thus required more food, in order to compensate. They also increased foraging on rainbow smelt, a species more readily available in the central part of the lake. The upshot of management of cormorants on Young Island was that more fish got eaten from Lake Champlain.

The rising moon shed a soft light across the water to end our banding for the night. We headed back toward the mainland, as I contemplated the challenges posed by trying to manage an ecosystem rather than a single species. Our inability to predict nature's responses to our management requires a constant willingness to adapt to new knowledge.

○ Dumpster Divers and Glorious Birds

"Dumpster divers." "Rats with wings." These are some of the insults casually hurled at gulls. Certainly, the dirty, unkempt look of the juveniles and their less than sanitary feeding habits lend themselves to such opprobrium. Yet, as I sit along the shore watching waves of snow-white gulls drift by, or study the crisp delineations of gray, white, and black on a handsome mature bird, or admire their graceful, effortless soaring, face-on to a stiff wind, I cannot help but feel great admiration for these birds.

Four species of gulls are typically seen throughout the year on Lake Champlain. None of them should technically be referred to as "sea" gulls, though commonly all are. Two species—ring-billed and herring—regularly nest around the lake. The other two species are more transient. Great black-backed gulls spend the winter on open water around the lake or its tributaries, though they do occasionally nest. Bonaparte's gulls pass through during migration, particularly in autumn.

Ring-billeds are currently our most common gull. Adults can be distinguished by the black band fully around their bill. Like most gulls, they eat anything they can get, though compared with the larger species, they tend to eat more insects. Ring-billeds, unlike our other gulls, frequently feed far from bodies of water. These are the birds that follow behind farm tractors, dropping down on insects and rodents stirred up by plowing or harvesting. Ornithologist Arthur Cleveland Bent, writing in 1921, considered the ring-billeds "as fully beneficial as any of the gulls" and a "gentle and harmless creature."

Formerly the most common gull on Lake Champlain, herring gulls now play second fiddle to the smaller ring-billeds. In addition to size differences, adult herring gulls can be distinguished by their yellow eye-ring and pink legs, compared to a red ring and yellow legs for the ring-billed. Herring gulls are also scavengers, though they focus more heavily on fish and are less likely than ring-billeds to forage in the uplands.

The largest gull encountered on Lake Champlain is the great black-backed. They can be seen at any season, though their numbers are highest during the winter. Bent compares these birds to eagles, saying of one, "its resemblance . . . was striking, as it soared aloft and wheeled in great circles, showing its broad black back and wings in sharp contrast with its snow-white head and tail, glistening in the sunlight." By dint of their great size they lord over smaller species, stealing food and defending space.

The Bonaparte's is the smallest gull regularly encountered on Lake Champlain. With their more delicate shape and habits, Bonapartes resemble terns, though their black-headed breeding plumage and absence of a forked tail serve to differentiate them. During the fall and winter the black head recedes to a black ear spot. On their breeding grounds to the north, Bonapartes make a habit of nesting in trees, in contrast to other gulls, who may occasionally use trees but prefer nesting on the ground.

The mix of gull species on Lake Champlain, and indeed throughout North America, has changed over time. Audubon described the ring-billed as the "Common American Gull" in 1840, just as it is today. However, during the late nineteenth and early twentieth century, ring-billed populations were decimated by egg collectors. By 1870, Edward Samuels, writing about the birds of New England, failed even to include the ring-billed. In contrast to the seeming ubiquity and ruggedness of the species today, Bent noted, "the ring-billed gull yields readily to persecution, is easily driven away from its breeding grounds, and seems to prefer to breed in remote, unsettled regions, far from the haunts of man."

Around the middle of the twentieth century, ring-billeds began to stage a comeback. Many factors probably influenced recovery, including protections enacted through the signing of the Migratory Bird Treaty of 1918, an end to plume and egg hunting, and the banning of DDT as of 1973. In 1949 the first nest was reported on Lake Champlain. Soon ring-billeds began displacing the larger herring gulls, which had persisted on the lake. The ring-billeds' propensity for feeding inland likely fostered their rapid population growth.

The population boom occurred beyond Lake Champlain. On the Great Lakes the ring-billed population reached 700,000 pairs after increasing an average of 11 percent per year from 1976 to 1984. Calls for population control became widespread. The Canadian Wildlife Service wrote at that time, "We do not yet know the limiting factors of the Great Lake ring-billed population."

Limiting factors are still not entirely evident, but they may have been met. On Lake Champlain the ring-billed population appears stable and probably has been since the mid-1990s. Perhaps the relatively recent influx of double-crested cormorants helped rein in the gulls' population growth. Perhaps reproductive rates have lowered. In the Great Lakes, industrial and household chemicals that impact hormonal control of development have been implicated in reducing breeding success by causing extra eggs in clutches, female-female pairing, and increased mortality of males.

Familiarity breeds contempt, and so it is in our relationship with gulls. But it need not be so. Rather, I prefer to recall Ruth Gordon's lines from the movie *Harold and Maude*: "Dreyfuss once wrote from Devil's Island that he had seen the most glorious birds. Many years later in Brittany he realized they had only been sea-gulls. For me, they will always be glorious birds."

○ Just Passing Through

Each October somewhere north of the Arctic Circle, flocks of white geese take flight on a journey. Over a five- or six-week period they cross Hudson Bay and land upon the Ungava Peninsula of northern Quebec. There they rest and refuel on roots and aquatic vegetation before taking off on a nonstop flight to Coopersville, New York, or Addison, Vermont, or any number of other cornfields throughout the Champlain Valley.

The arrival of the snow geese is a spectacle: the raucous honking of tens of thousands of birds in a field; the skeins streaming across the sky; the aerial acrobatics—rolls and flips—as the birds spill air off their wings when coming in to land. Cars line the sides of roads, as even tepid nature fans become enraptured by the noisy fields of white.

The cornfields act like a gas station along the birds' highway system from north to south. By the time they arrive, the corn has been harvested and is in the barn, but waste kernels remain to provide fuel for the remainder of the birds' trip. Most of the geese feed for a few days or a week before continuing on their journey to wintering grounds along the Atlantic Ocean from New Jersey south through the Carolinas. A few linger until snow covers the fields.

Though the snow geese are the most visible flocks of birds to pass through the Lake Champlain basin, they are by no means the only ones. Lake Champlain serves as a vital migration route in the Atlantic Flyway, a broad geographic area through which many birds pass during their seasonal travels. The Atlantic Flyway is one of four recognized

Lake Champlain serves as a vital migration route in the Atlantic flyway. (photo by Trip Kinney)

in the United States. Within each flyway migrating birds tend to follow natural features such as mountain ranges, coastlines, and rivers, especially if the features are oriented in the direction the birds want to go. To them, Lake Champlain, stretching as it does from north to south, is a natural connection between the St. Lawrence River and the Atlantic Coast. All told, over 250 species of birds can be found in the basin in a given year, attracted by the diversity and abundance of habitats.

Shorebirds begin moving through the area in August. Like the snow geese, they begin their journey from the Arctic, but some will migrate as far as the coast of South America. Most shorebirds seek out muddy areas along the lake's margin or inland to probe for worms and other invertebrates. Low lake levels mean a food bonanza for them.

In September warblers head south from their local haunts and from points north. Though many species migrate at night, mixed flocks can be seen dancing through lakeshore forests hunting insects. At this time of year these bright, showy denizens of the treetops have molted to duller plumages, making species identification challenging.

Also in September, broad-winged hawk migration reaches its peak, and thousands can pass in a single day. While other hawks move through in small groups, the bulk of the broad-wing migration takes place in a very concentrated period. On a sunny day following a cold front, the hawks take advantage of thermal updrafts created by warm air rising in currents off the ridges of mountains. Once a bird finds a good thermal, others soon join it, forming a kettle. The warm air lifts the birds high into the sky. After gaining altitude they can glide for long distances using very little energy. Open

Common loon in Meach Cove (photo by Trip Kinney)

ridgelines facing east from the Adirondacks or west from the Green Mountains provide prime viewing areas for hawk-watching, but observers need good eyes and strong binoculars to spot the most distant birds against a bright blue background of sky.

Long strings of crows can be seen streaming south in November. Sometimes these flocks stretch for miles. Though we usually think of crows as being resident year-round, they too have their seasonal movements.

October is for ducks. For most of the summer, when one spies a bird swimming on the lake or flying above it, there is a high probability it will be a gull or cormorant. Sure, there are occasional mergansers with their loon-shaped bodies; and mallards can always be found somewhere. On a year-round average these two species are probably the most common, but through the summer at least, they stay hidden and so are less visible than gulls and cormorants. Then in the autumn, with the responsibility of laying eggs and rearing young behind them, waterfowl begin their journey to wintering grounds. One can find twice as many duck species in December in the basin as during the breeding season.

I once spent a crisp autumn morning at Thompson's Point in Charlotte, Vermont. Northward from there the Main Lake broadened and stretched to the horizon. The Four Brothers hovered just above the plane of the lake in a haze of distorted air. The ferry plied its way back and forth between Charlotte and Essex. A flock of twenty or so birds passed on the opposite shoreline with long necks, dark heads, and flashing wings set against a backdrop of the turning foliage's oranges and reds.

"Brant," yelled out a voice from behind one of the spotting scopes clustered on the point, scanning the lake. Brant resemble Canada geese but are smaller and darker. Where Canadas have a white patch on the chin to separate the black of the head and neck, the brant's head and neck appear all black at a distance.

By the end of the morning dozens of brant had passed, along with even greater numbers of white-winged scoters skimming just above the surface of the lake in tight pods. With a strong north wind, the numbers could climb into the hundreds or perhaps even thousands for the two species. And yet, few people on Lake Champlain ever see these birds, most of which do not stop to feed or laze in the fields like snow geese. Instead they follow the lake like a roadway to the Atlantic Coast. For these birds, Thompson's Point formed the neck of a funnel, like traffic being condensed from three lanes to one on a busy interstate.

As inland ponds and northern areas freeze, their winged inhabitants congregate on Lake Champlain. Then, as Champlain's ice grows, the birds become easier to find because they are concentrated in smaller and smaller areas. Pockets of open water can host multiple species.

Perhaps the greatest difference between winter and summer duck concentrations is the sheer number of goldeneye on the lake in winter. Goldeneye, or whistlers, are chunky diving ducks with graceful plumage—white bodies and dark wings and head with a spot of white in the cheek area at the base of the bill. These cavity nesters have occasionally been documented as raising young in the Champlain Valley, but the bulk of their breeding grounds lie to the north. Yet in winter they are perhaps the most common bird on the lake. Great flocks gather in protected bays, feeding and loafing. Toward spring, one can observe a male's mating display where he snaps his head onto his back as if his neck had just come unhinged.

In addition to the ducks and geese, grebes and loons are also easier to find in winter. Loons can be seen at any time of year, but they are more common in the colder months. Individuals on the lake in the summer are usually unmated juveniles biding their time until they can gain a territory on a smaller pond. Lake Champlain's high waves, boat traffic, and rocky or steep shorelines make it less than ideal for loon breeding. They prefer calmer waters. Grebes are ducklike diving birds with lobed rather than webbed feet. Horned grebes are the most common winter species, while pied-billed grebes breed sporadically in the basin.

By the end of December most of the winter movements are complete, and species settle in for the season. Many birds from the Arctic, like snow buntings and rough-legged hawks, come here to escape the cold, while human residents of the area start thinking of their own southern migration.

Thus Lake Champlain provides food and shelter not just for the permanent denizens of the basin but also for those birds just passing through. There is a wide diversity of bird life out there, but not at convenient times. Frigid winter days offer rafts of diving ducks; wind-whipped autumn mornings promise flocks of numerous birds sneaking through the valley on a longer voyage; while spring and summer birds concentrate their displays in the early morning hours. There is certainly more than just gulls and cormorants.

○ Links in the Chain

The well-known children's song about a lady who swallowed a fly ran through my head after my wife brought home a book version from the library for our toddler. If you remember the song, the old lady goes on to swallow a spider to eat the fly, a rat to eat the spider, a cat to chase the rat, and so on and so on. The song paints a whimsical picture of a string of mouths through which food may pass—a food chain. It's a concept so simple a child can understand it, but like so many phenomena in nature, the concept gets increasingly less clear, and more interesting, as you scratch its surface.

Food chains in real life are substantially shorter than the one stretching into the old lady's gullet to get her fly. With each transfer of food, some of the energy captured therein is lost. For example, it might take a pound of seed to make an ounce of mouse—one step on the food chain. It then takes a pound of mouse to make an ounce of fox—the second step. The availability of mice limits the number of foxes that can exist in an area, and without abundant foxes there is no way to have a predator large enough to live on fox meat. Food chains seldom extend more than three or four links, at least on land.

In lakes, food chains can stretch up to five and sometimes even six links. Fish are more efficient at converting energy from their prey into mass that can be eaten by other fish, because they use less of the energy they consume to regulate their body temperature, relying instead upon the heat-holding capacity of the water in which they live. Air temperature is much more volatile than water temperature, so the fish strategy doesn't work for large terrestrial carnivores.

However, food chain length can vary even between different lakes, and the reasons for this have been the subject of much debate. Two factors that have been thought to control the length of food chains in lakes are the productivity and the size of the systems. The productivity of the lake is measured by the amount of solar energy it can capture. Highly productive lakes have lots of nutrients, convert lots of sunlight into biomass, and as a result are covered with carpets of algae and plants. Hypothetically, the ability to capture energy should be translated into more energy available for more food chain links. Alternatively, larger lakes could allow more food chain links by having more species or more available habitat or more complex habitats.

Testing these hypotheses is challenging. One can't simply throw on scuba gear and follow a fish around until it gets eaten and then continue following its predator, and so on. However, researchers at Cornell University and the Institute of Ecosystem Studies found a way to get around that problem.

Apparently, certain isotopes of nitrogen accumulate with each link in the food chain, while concentrations of carbon isotopes remain constant between links. By collecting samples from top predators and comparing accumulating forms of nitrogen to more common forms and to carbon, the researchers could determine how many steps in the food chain lie below the top predator. They collected samples from twenty-five lakes in the Northeast (including Champlain) across a variety of sizes and productivity levels and compared the results.

Their findings? The productivity of a lake had no impact on how many links there were, but lake size was a strong predictor of food chain length—larger lakes have longer food chains. The researchers speculated as to why large lakes might have more links, but that is a question for another study.

The length of a food chain has practical implications for consumers of fish. Just as some types of nitrogen accumulate in the food chain, so too do some pollutants. PCBs and mercury in particular are found in extremely low concentrations in the water column but increase in the flesh of fish, reaching their highest concentrations in top predators. If food chains on large lakes have more links, then toxic concentrations are also likely to be higher in top predators from big lakes.

The old lady who swallowed a fly eventually swallowed a horse, and thus met a gruesome fate for a children's book (she died). Few people eat enough fish from large or small lakes to worry about a similar fate from ingesting PCBs or mercury, though the possibility of sublethal effects has received relatively little attention. There are populations clearly at risk, most notably children and women of childbearing age who might accumulate contaminants and pass them to their babies. New York and Vermont both recommend these groups eat none of the top predators from Lake Champlain (walleye and lake trout). For others, limiting meals of fresh fish to once per month is a prudent safety precaution.

○ Something Fishy

For many people Lake Champlain means fishing, and fishing means lake trout and salmon, smallmouth bass and perch, walleye and pickerel, catfish and sunfish—but these represent only the tip of fish diversity. Lake Champlain hosts about seventy species of fish, and an additional dozen or so species inhabit tributaries between the fall lines and the lake. However, few people could name more than a third of them. Even fewer could say anything about their habitats and needs.

Following the retreat of the glaciers, fish colonized Lake Champlain from refuges along the Atlantic Coast and from the Great Lakes / Mississippi drainage basin. A few species had survived the glaciers in eastern refuges, most of which are now likely under the ocean. These species migrated into what was then Lake Vermont via the Hudson River. Additionally, they could have come through what is now the Connecticut River, because for a period of 1,000 years the Winooski River drained east, owing to an ice dam at its western mouth. Fish that accessed the Winooski during this time could then enter Lake Champlain once the river began flowing west.

Most of Lake Champlain's fish species came from the Great Lakes. There were three separate opportunities for migration. For a period both the Great Lakes and Lake Vermont emptied to the Atlantic via the Hudson River. Later, even after the Great Lakes drained to the St. Lawrence River, ice prevented a northern escape, and so the water moved southward through Lake Vermont. Finally, after the Champlain Sea became fresh water, the outlet of the Great Lakes drainage was still high enough that fish could move between that system and Lake Champlain. A few species were able to adapt to a freshwater existence after entering the lake during the Champlain Sea stage. More important of late, humans have moved species between different water bodies either intentionally, as in the case of brown trout, or accidentally, as in the case of alewives.

The most diverse family of fish in the lake are the cyprinids, a category that includes minnows, shiners, and dace. There are eighteen species of cyprinids in the lake, and another six between the lake and the first upstream falls that acts as a barrier—nearly three times the number of species as the next largest group. The largest of the cyprinids, carp and goldfish, have been introduced from elsewhere, but most of the native species never exceed five inches in length.

Much of the challenge in understanding these smaller species comes from limited opportunities for observing them. Any long-term observational studies must be done in controlled laboratory settings where natural variability is excluded—a quite unrealistic scenario. Population surveys are limited by our means of sampling the populations. Some species may behaviorally avoid minnow traps. Nets are limited by their mesh size or our ability to deploy them. Population distributions vary seasonally, daily, or at different life stages of the fish. Since minnows and other small fish lack the sporting appeal of larger species, many questions remain unanswered.

Doug Facey, a biologist at St. Michael's College in Colchester, works to understand how some of the lesser-known species use Lake Champlain and the lower, deep, slow-moving reaches of its larger tributaries. To do so, he first tries to assess which species are there. I joined him on the Missisquoi River one day.

We began by running seine nets along the shoreline. Seines consist of a net strung between two poles. One person stands on either end, and the net is moved through the habitat to be sampled. However, along the Missisquoi the water becomes deep quite rapidly, and there are few places where seine nets can be safely deployed. In our case one individual stayed on shore and the second waded out as far as was feasible. We then moved parallel to shore, dragging the net along the bottom. As I worked the water end of the net, my feet continually slipped along the silty bottom toward deeper water, urged on by the pressure of water against my waders. Seine nets are effective at sampling smaller species because they have a fairly fine mesh. We seined twice in weedy areas and twice along sandy river bends, collecting a total of eight species, including well-known species like yellow perch and smallmouth bass, and some lesser-known but common species like the tessellated darter and bluntnose minnow.

We spent some extra time searching for and finding eastern sand darters. Both New York and Vermont have recognized that the sand darters' limited habitat affinities make them vulnerable and so have listed the species as threatened. These pinky-size translucent fish of the perch family burrow into sandy substrates on large, slow-moving rivers or along lakes. Presumably burrowing helps them avoid predators and conceal themselves from prey. However, even within a given sandbar, the darters may occupy only a small area with ideal-size substrate, according to Facey.

After seining we collected three fyke nets that Facey had set out the previous day. Fyke nets consist of a series of hula hoop–like rings with net strung between them. Fish swim through the first ring, which is the largest, and are then guided forward through smaller rings. Once the fish pass through the last ring, they can't turn back, because of the presence of a series of funnels. The nets can catch any fish small enough to swim through the rings but miss those so small they slip through the mesh. Fyke nets can be left overnight, whereas the seine net captures fish only in the area at the time of sampling. Our fykes were filled with channel catfish, smallmouth bass, rock bass, pumpkinseeds, and yellow perch. Previously, Facey had also caught some large bowfins—heavy, hard-fighting fish with a dorsal fin that runs along most of their back.

On a separate occasion I joined Bernie Pientka and his crew from the Vermont Fish & Wildlife Department as they used a large seine to take samples on Missisquoi Bay. Groaning and creaking from the back of a pickup truck, a winch would spool a cable pulling in the net three days a week, three times a day, for over a month. By the time it reached shore, the net had passed through approximately thirteen acres of Missisquoi Bay, and the winch seemed tired. As the net neared shore, Pientka waded into the water and hauled it to land. He and his crew pulled out flapping perch, bluegill, suckers, bullhead, northern pike, and sorted them.

Every five years since 1985 the department has sampled the fish population at the same spot with the same methods. It started as an attempt to assess the walleye population in the bay, but lately attention has been given to nongame species as well. The resulting data help us better understand changes in the Missisquoi Bay food chain.

Missisquoi Bay often hosts extensive summer algae blooms. The bay's problems even prompted coverage by the *Washington Post* in 2004. Managers have long known that algae blooms require nutrients, and control efforts have focused on reducing nutrient loading. The influence of nutrients is referred to as a "bottom-up" effect. Nutrients start at the bottom of the food chain but affect higher links. However, in the last fifteen years, a different species of toxin-producing algae has come to dominate Missisquoi Bay, even in the absence of any detectable change in nutrient concentrations.

What if there are "top-down" factors driving part of the change in algae? In other words, to what extent can higher food-chain links influence lower links? European research published in 2004 in the journal *Freshwater Biology* determined that the effects of changes in the fish community on lake ecosystems were substantial, even though nutrients exerted a stronger effect. Furthermore, fish and nutrients had an approximately equal effect on zooplankton—organisms that eat algae and are eaten by fish.

The theoretical basis for "top-down" effects is well established. However, in order for managers to determine if or how such effects might influence algae in Missisquoi Bay, they first must determine what changes have actually occurred in the fish community. There is a wide range of suspected changes that could lead to top-down effects. Walleye sit at the top of the food chain, and declines in the species have long disturbed lake watchers. In April 1983 the Lake Champlain Committee newsletter noted, "There has been concern from anglers in Vermont, as well as fishery people, that the Walleye fishery in Lake Champlain does not exist in the quality or quantity it did 20 years ago." Also, numerous northern pike and their kin, another group of top predators, have been stricken with a viral disease that leaves their skin covered with red pussy lesions. The disease was virtually unknown in the lake prior to 2002.

In the middle food chain, white perch are a recent arrival in the bay. Surveyors in the Quebec portion of the bay first documented the species in the winter of 2000–2001. By 2003 white perch were the dominant species, with three times more of them than yellow perch. The diets of white and yellow perch can overlap at times, and white perch are highly competitive foragers.

One weakness of sampling only once every five years is that some aspects of Pientka's data are difficult to interpret. For example, the low number of walleye in a given year's sample might be because ice-out came late and the fish were already on their spawning grounds before netting could begin.

Other information is clear. Pientka's work documented zebra mussels in the bay for the first time ever. Though zebra mussels had colonized most of the lake years earlier, and planktonic juveniles had been found in the bay, his record of adults was noteworthy. Missisquoi Bay has less calcium for zebra mussel shells than other parts of the lake, and it had been thought that this might be sufficient to keep them out. However, between 1 and 3 percent of the mussels brought in by the nets as a by-product of collecting fish were zebra mussels. They, too, could change the bay's food chain.

Changes in sport fish populations in the lake, real or perceived, galvanize ardent concern. Have walleye declined? Why are there so many sea lamprey on the lake trout and salmon? Where are the yellow perch? Such questions, though, ignore the forage base, the small fish, assuming they will always be there and that one forage fish is as good as the next. However, with the introduction of more than a dozen species of nonnative fish, and with so little known about the habits and habitats of the species we have, such assumptions should not be taken for granted.

○ Fish Flu

The beginning of each cold and flu season seems to bring word of some worrisome new germ. Certainly diseases have been important, often underappreciated shapers of our world. Epidemics like the Spanish flu in 1918, the Asian flu of 1956, and the Hong Kong flu of 1968 killed millions. In the last few years the media have been filled with stories about new viruses that cause bird flu and SARS (severe acute respiratory syndrome). Of course, humans aren't the only animals that must battle with novel infectious agents; diseases can shape fish populations, too.

Early in June 2001, numerous dead fish washed ashore in the South Lake. Most were white crappie, but there were a few other species and also some map turtles. They were victims of a fairly common bacterium, *Flexibacter columnaris*, that typically causes a low-grade annoying condition. However, when Columnaris disease, as it is called, is coupled with stressful conditions, it can be lethal. The die-off had been preceded by an unseasonable warm spell in early May, during the spawning season, followed by a frigid period, conditions that likely weakened the fish.

Lately, other diseases have been found that are relatively new to the affected populations. Although not yet in Lake Champlain, whirling disease has been identified in scattered locations in New York since at least 1994 and in the Batten Kill of southern Vermont since 2001. The parasite that causes whirling disease reproduces in the head and spinal cartilage of young trout. The pressure it creates causes the fish to swim erratically, thus the disease's name. According to the U.S. Fish and Wildlife Service, the parasite first arrived in North America from Europe in the 1950s. It has generated a great deal of concern for the health of trout fisheries, particularly in the West, but the actual threat to wild fish populations is unknown.

In 2002, northern pike with large white growths on their skin began appearing in Missisquoi Bay. The condition was eventually determined to be an esocid lymphosarcoma, likely caused by a virus. The disease has been known for over eighty years in both Europe and North America, but it had not been reported in Lake Champlain previously. It seems to be most prevalent during the spawning period in late winter and early spring, decreasing in frequency and severity as the water warms. As with most diseases, the extent to which infected fish can survive is unclear, but fish with healed-over scars have been observed in recent years.

The latest disease to cause concern is viral hemorrhagic septicemia (VHS). The first recorded outbreaks in North America occurred in salt water, but in 2005, die-offs attributed to VHS occurred in Michigan and Ontario. The disease was found in Lake Ontario and the St. Lawrence Seaway during the summer of 2006.

VHS affects a wide variety of fish species, and its presence has led to stricter regulation of fish transfers. There is now a federal order prohibiting the importation of many species of live fish from Ontario, Quebec, and the eight states bordering the Great Lakes. In June 2007 New York state instituted permanent rules that would prohibit commercial collection of baitfish from waters where VHS has been identified, limit the number of baitfish that can be possessed for personal use to one hundred and restrict their use to the water body where they were caught, and require any live fish scheduled for release to undergo health inspections. In October 2007 Vermont enacted emergency rules to curb the spread of VHS and has since developed permanent regulations.

Like whirling disease, VHS is not native to North America but rather has spread from Europe. These two diseases are a reminder that invasive exotic species come in all forms and types. Those that are best known, like zebra mussels and water chestnut, represent only a fraction of the total.

People can prepare for cold and flu season with shots, but even then, new strains occasionally cause terrible damage. Fish are also subject to new disease strains, but they do not have the luxury of shots. As with all invasive exotics, preventing the spread and establishment of disease organisms, and thus protecting fish species, requires care and vigilance. The New York Department of Environmental Conservation has prepared a list of steps (see box) that individuals can take to ensure they are not responsible for spreading diseases to new locations.

Guidelines to Prevent the Spread of Fish Disease

- Remove all mud, aquatic plants and animals from all gear, boats, motors, and trailers before leaving a body of water.

- Drain your live well, bilge, and bait tanks before leaving the fishing or boating water. Anglers or boaters using infected waters should disinfect their live wells and bait wells with a 10 percent chlorine/water solution. Rinse well to remove all residual chlorine.

- Do not transport fish from one body of water to another. Note that this practice is illegal without a DEC fish-stocking permit.

- Only use baitfish in the water body it was taken from. Bait purchased commercially should not be released into any body of water.

- Do not dispose of fish carcasses or by-products in any body of water.

Source: New York State Department of Environmental Conservation.

○ Salmonid Challenges

Between raising and stocking of four different species of salmonids (rainbow trout, brown trout, lake trout, and Atlantic salmon) and ongoing sea lamprey management, no wildlife program on Lake Champlain requires as much input as that of salmonids. Somewhere near the end of the nineteenth century, lake trout (called "lakers") disappeared from Lake Champlain, due perhaps to a combination of overfishing and development in the watershed. Around the same time, Atlantic salmon also disappeared, though whether the lake's population had been sea-run fish or landlocked is disputed. Ever since then, efforts have been made to restore these populations, with only minimal success. Some of the impediments were foreseen—for example, high sea lamprey populations decrease the survival rate of stocked fish. Some challenges are new, such as the arrival and spread of alewives. Still other impediments to restoring a healthy self-propagating population remain a mystery.

The Known: Sea Lamprey

Lamprey are among the most primitive organisms with backbones, their basic body structure having evolved much earlier than most other vertebrates. The key clue to their early origins is the lack of a jaw. The evolution of a jaw was a pivotal event in vertebrate development. It greatly expanded the means by which food could be obtained and manipulated, and allowed organisms to better defend themselves. Without a jaw, lampreys' feeding strategies are limited. As young, the animals reside in bottom sediments and filter pollen, algae, and other organic matter. In many species these young then transform into juveniles that attach to fish with their suckerlike mouth, rasp a hole in the side of the prey, and drain its bodily fluids. The small scales of trout and salmon are easier to penetrate than larger scales of bass.

Sea lamprey, the best known species in the group, exhibit a fascinating life cycle. Individuals survive for four to seven years, though they spend only the final year as parasites. Spawning adults move into streams in the spring to mate and lay eggs. At this time they are no longer capable of feeding. Upon arrival at spawning grounds they use their mouths to gather small stones into nests, and each female lays tens of thousands of eggs, only a small percentage of which hatch. Once the blind larvae hatch, they drift downstream into quiet reaches, where they burrow into sediments and filter feed. They spend three to six years in this stage. At some point the larvae metamorphose, growing eyes and developing a new digestive track and mouth parts. They then move to the lake, where they spend twelve to twenty months feeding on other fish, before returning to spawn. They do not seem to have fidelity to their stream of origin and in recent years have been found in more and more streams around the basin.

For many years sea lamprey were thought to be an exotic organism in Lake Champlain and the Great Lakes. Up and down the Atlantic Coast, sea lamprey spawn in freshwater rivers but then spend most of their lives in salt water. They arrived in Lake Erie after the Welland Canal connected it to Lake Ontario and, by extension, the St. Lawrence Seaway, in 1921 (about twenty years after lake trout had been extirpated from Lake Champlain). From there they spread to Lakes Michigan, Huron, and Superior, and it became generally assumed that freshwater populations of saltwater lamprey must be exotic.

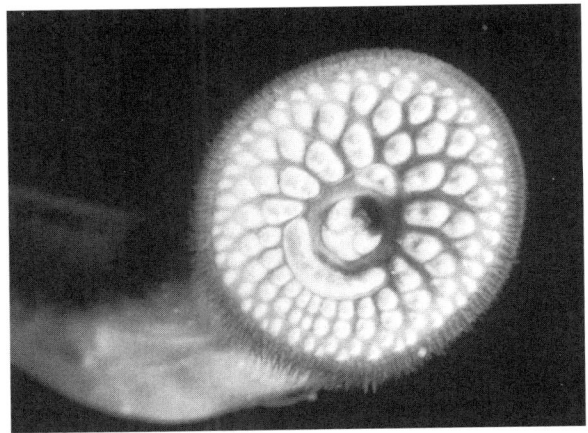

Sea lamprey (photo: U.S. Fish and Wildlife Service)

More recently, however, genetic research suggested that sea lamprey are actually native to some freshwater bodies, including Lake Champlain, Lake Ontario, and Cayuga Lake in New York. The researchers found significant differences in the genetic structure of sea lamprey in these lakes compared to those in the upper Great Lakes. Those in the upper Great Lakes had been established from a few colonizers relatively recently. Those in Champlain, Ontario, and Cayuga had been isolated for a substantial period of time. Meanwhile, sea lamprey along the Atlantic Coast consisted of one giant population. Such differences suggest that the lamprey in Lake Champlain had likely become established when the lake held a saltwater sea following the last glaciation.

Though sea lamprey are the best-known species, there are at least two other lamprey species in the Champlain basin: silver lamprey, American brook lamprey, and northern brook lamprey. (Yes, I said *two* species—but more on that later). Silver lamprey, like sea lamprey, are parasitic as adults. They are about two-thirds the size of sea lamprey, but the two species' habitats and life cycles overlap considerably. The two brook lamprey do not parasitize fish. In fact they do not even feed as adults; rather they transform, reproduce, and die. Brook lamprey also differ in being half as big as even silver lamprey, and they do not migrate to the lake. Both these species have a much more limited distribution than their parasitic kin.

In the Great Lakes region a decline in populations of silver lamprey and northern brook lamprey has been noted, leading to concerns about the species and expanded research as to their habitat requirements. Though adults are quite different, as larvae these two lampreys are indistinguishable, so investigators tried to use genetic clues to identify larval specimens. However, they ran into a problem. There does not seem to be any genetic differences between them. The only conclusion the investigators could reach was that silver lamprey and northern brook lamprey are actually two variations of the same species.

In 1990 New York, Vermont, and the federal government began a joint eight-year experimental program to control sea lamprey on Lake Champlain. Pesticides were added to streams and deltas where young lamprey develop. On some smaller streams, spawning adults were trapped to prevent reproduction from occurring. The experimental program achieved reductions in the number of sea lamprey wounds on fish, and management agencies considered it successful. In 2001 a full-scale ongoing program was begun, though results to date have been less satisfying. As of 2007, pesticides or trapping have been used on eighteen stream systems and five deltas throughout the basin, and the agencies involved intend to expand efforts to other streams.

The New: Alewives

In the summer of 1997 while working in Lake St. Catherine in Poultney, Vermont Fish & Wildlife officials found a different kind of fish. Later analysis confirmed that it was the first appearance of alewives in the Lake Champlain basin. By 2005, alewives were confirmed in Lake Champlain by Vermont fisheries biologists, first around Grand Isle, then later throughout the lake.

Alewives feed primarily on plankton and were named for their swollen abdomen, which reminded some of the girth of women who kept taverns. Under natural conditions alewives live in salt water, migrating to fresh water only to breed. Along the coast of Maine the absence of alewives returning to streams where they were once abundant has been a concern.

Alewife (photo by Shawn Good, Vermont Fish & Wildlife Department)

Sometimes, as in Lake Champlain, alewives establish a self-sustaining population in fresh water, where their presence is less welcome. It happened in the Great Lakes about 150 years ago. The fish probably traveled through the Erie Canal, a population became entrenched in Lake Ontario, and now alewives constitute the bulk of the diet for trout and salmon in the Great Lakes.

Their importance in the Great Lakes food web may have led an imprudent angler to think that alewives in Lake Champlain would be a boon to salmonids here—a less than sound strategy. Though alewives can be a food source for adult fish, they also feed on eggs and juveniles of those same species. As if eating the young were not enough, there is also thiaminase.

Alewives produce a lot of an enzyme, thiaminase, that interferes with assimilation of thiamin (vitamin B_1). As a result, trout that eat alewives lack sufficient thiamin, which leads to very high mortality in the trout's offspring. So much for any benefits from another forage fish.

The importance of the alewife introduction to Lake Champlain extends beyond the potentially harmful effects on salmonid reproduction. In the Great Lakes, alewife populations go through tremendous boom-and-bust cycles. When things are booming, all is well, but when busts occur, the results are downright revolting. Wave after wave of dead alewives wash up on shore. Literally, tons of dead fish have to be cleared from beaches. Lake Champlain saw its first large-scale alewife die-off in the spring of 2008.

Alewives have not yet been in Lake Champlain long enough for scientists to assess their impact with any certainty. However, their potential for wreaking havoc is comparable to that of an earlier invader, zebra mussels. The introduction of zebra mussels in the early 1990s probably had a greater impact on lake ecology than any management practice undertaken. Zebra mussels have colonized the majority of the lake, smothered native mussels, provided refuges for some plankton species while selectively feeding on others, and provided a food source for some fish species while making it harder for other species to feed. Perhaps the most notable impact of zebra mussels is their ability to increase water clarity by filtering out particles in the water column. Increased clarity has been a mixed blessing, improving aesthetics but allowing weeds like Eurasian water milfoil and water chestnut to grow at greater depths than previously.

In order to understand how alewives might impact Lake Champlain, we can turn to other lakes where they have become established. Otsego Lake, at the headwaters of the Susquehanna River near Cooperstown, New York, has some of the best data on ecosystem conditions before and after the introduction of alewives. Compared to Lake Champlain, Otsego is tiny; Champlain's Main Lake alone is twenty-four times larger than Otsego and its entire watershed. Nonetheless, the lake does have some similarities to Champlain. Both were carved by glaciers and are relatively deep for their surface area. The population density in the two drainage basins is nearly identical, about sixty-eight people per square mile. Additionally, residents around both lakes have struggled to manage nuisance algae blooms.

Alewives arrived on Otsego Lake in 1986. Prior to that, cisco (also called lake herring) were the dominant consumers of plankton, as rainbow smelt currently are in Lake Champlain. By 1991 alewives were abundant, and within a decade of introduction they had outcompeted the cisco, whose population crashed. Rainbow smelt, which had been introduced to Otsego less than ten years before alewives, essentially disappeared as well.

The incredible competitive ability of alewives derives from their unusual feeding mechanisms. Rainbow smelt and cisco are visual predators. That means their plankton prey must be large enough to be seen, and the fish then expend energy chasing the prey. While alewives do locate prey by sight, they also can passively gather prey. In the absence of large plankton, alewives swim with their mouths open. As water passes over their gills, they collect and feed on small prey that other planktivores cannot utilize.

Because of their feeding efficiency, alewives were able to change the community composition of the Otsego Lake plankton. The mass of the largest plankton class decreased by 80 percent, and the average size of the largest individuals in that class decreased by more than half. Fewer plankton meant fewer algae were filtered from the water, and the concentration of algae increased almost three times. Correspondingly, water clarity decreased markedly. All the efforts that watershed groups had spent trying to limit nutrient loading in an attempt to control algae were offset with the introduction of a nonnative fish. (On the positive side, the number of lake trout increased, as they fed on the alewives, though researchers from other lakes have not seen similar increases, likely because of thiaminase.)

Incredible numbers of walleye have been stocked in Otsego Lake in an attempt to control alewives. Fingerlings are placed in the lake during alewives' spawning period. The results have been encouraging: the walleye are doing well; the algae have decreased; zooplankton are returning; water clarity has increased slightly; and the average size of alewives has decreased slightly. Other lakes have also attempted to control alewives by stocking walleye, but results have been mixed.

One somewhat counterintuitive finding from Otsego Lake was that the alewife population declines noticeably following mild winters. It is well known that alewives are sensitive to temperature. They avoid waters colder than 34 degrees Fahrenheit. In years following exceptionally warm Mays and Junes (their spawning period), there will be more alewives. Thus, intuitively, one would expect bitterly cold winters to decrease alewife populations—but that does not happen. Rather, bitter cold causes the lake to freeze, thus insulating the lower depths. In mild years when ice does not form, winds stir the lake all winter long, distributing the cold water throughout the system.

Using the lessons of Otsego Lake to predict the effects of alewives in Lake Champlain is not straightforward. There are examples of lakes where alewives have arrived but not flourished, including Lake Erie, Lake Superior, and Oneida Lake, but the reasons for the alewives' lack of success in these lakes are unknown. Since Lake Champlain is less likely to freeze than Otsego Lake, perhaps that would bode ill for alewives. However, Champlain has numerous large, shallow bays that do freeze. Perhaps the alewives will find seasonal refuge in Missisquoi Bay or the South Lake before returning to the Main Lake after spawning. Most intriguing, zebra mussels preceded alewives in Lake Champlain, and zebra mussels also filter plankton, providing a source of competition that alewives didn't face when colonizing the Great Lakes or Otsego Lake.

Though Otsego Lake can help us anticipate what might happen with alewives on Champlain and guide us in evaluating the impacts, each situation is unique. The one unambiguous lesson is that it is better to prevent an invasion from a new exotic than to try to cope with it after the fact.

The Mystery: Where Are the Young?

One impediment to lake trout restoration that still mystifies managers is the failure of the fish to survive from hatching to adulthood. An observation in the late 1990s led to identification of the problem. Over 90 percent of the fish being recaptured in the lake bore fin clips, the mark of being reared in a hatchery. After having stocked over five million fish in the lake, having spent seven years controlling sea lamprey populations, and despite a thriving adult laker population that appeared to be spawning each year, for some reason lake managers were finding very few fish born in the lake surviving to be captured. Somewhere along the line, the lake trout disappeared.

Enter Dr. Ellen Marsden and her graduate student Brian Ellrott. In the summer of 2000 they began a series of systematic observations and experiments with the purpose of identifying the life stage at which lake trout disappeared. They identified fourteen potential spawning locations in the lake, searched them for potential egg predators, and collected spawned trout eggs at five sites. Later, they returned to sites where they knew the trout had spawned and collected recently hatched fish (known as fry). They also towed trawl nets along the bottom of Shelburne, Whallon, and Willsboro bays in search of juvenile lake trout.

Their results offered clues as to the age at which lakers disappeared. It was not the eggs; they found eggs at eight of the fourteen sites, indicating successful spawning occurred. Additionally, those eggs were hatching, as evidenced by fry at three of the five sites sampled. Thus, even though egg predators were present, they were not eating everything. Best of all, the density of both eggs and fry were higher than in parts of Lake Huron where naturally self-sustaining populations of lake trout do exist. The problem seemed to be with the juveniles. Only in Shelburne Bay did they find any juvenile fish, and those had all been stocked.

Now, the absence of juveniles in bottom trawls does not provide unequivocal evidence that the missing life stage had been identified. The number of trawls and their geographic extent were fairly limited. Perhaps the fish were somewhere else at the time of the surveys—in a different part of the lake, or at a different water depth. However, absence of juveniles, coupled with the relatively large number of eggs produced, the prevalence of fry, and the survival of stocked fish, provided a strong suggestion that an important key to solving the mystery had been identified.

The next question, and one for which answers have not yet been found, is why are the fish disappearing? Sea lamprey, the typical bogeyman, are unlikely to target these small fish. Marsden and Ellrott offered three potential mechanisms that could account for the missing fish: perhaps some contaminants were hindering development and growth; perhaps some predator was decimating the population; or perhaps there was some disease in the lake that struck young fish.

Marsden and another graduate student, Jake Riley, have since investigated the impacts of predation on lake trout fry. First, they needed to figure out who might be eating the young lakers. They trapped a number of potential predators, including rock bass, yellow perch, and burbot, during the period when lake trout fry hatch on spawning reefs, and examined the content of the predators' stomachs. Their tentative conclusion was that everybody eats laker fry—though they were still not certain whether the amount of predation is sufficient to explain the near-complete absence of fry advancing to the adult life stage. Additionally, fry raised under controlled conditions showed no signs of disease. As yet, there is no evidence to suggest or refute any impacts from contaminants.

Restoring lake trout via stocking has had mixed results. In Lakes Huron and Superior, stocking was successful, and populations now sustain themselves. In Lakes Michigan and Champlain, stocking has not resulted in self-sustaining populations. The reason in Lake Michigan seems fairly straightforward: high density of egg predators coupled with a low number of spawners means not enough eggs hatch. In Lake Champlain the impediment to successfully producing adult lakers is still unknown but likely occurs between the time eggs hatch and adults spawn. While stocked fish still spawn, those born in the lake disappear while still juveniles. For now, if Lake Champlain is to host any lakers, they must be replenished annually, and restoration of natural predator-prey dynamics in the lake remains out of reach.

◯ Holding an Eel by the Tail

The warm, salty Sargasso Sea seems as distant in character from the chill of a Lake Champlain winter as one could get while still being wet. Encircled by North Atlantic currents, the Sargasso stretches from the Greater Antilles in the Caribbean north to Bermuda and east to the Azores. It's an area famous for calm weather and thick growths of seaweed in very deep water. It's also the birthing grounds of one of Lake Champlain's more interesting denizens—the American eel.

These days one mostly hears the term "eel" or "eel-like" used to describe sea lamprey, and superficially the long, sleek bodies of the sea lamprey and the American eel do resemble each other; but in fact there is little relationship between the two species. While both are considered fish in that they are water-dwelling vertebrates with gills, the lamprey's lack of jaws puts it in a class apart from other fishes and most vertebrates.

For eons, billions of larval eels would leave the Sargasso Sea each year and drift in the currents of the Gulf Stream. After about a year had passed, the larvae would develop a greater ability to swim for themselves. For some this development might occur in the vicinity of the Gulf of St. Lawrence, and they would break free and head into the estuary of the river. There, they would settle and feed for a time. With each tidal surge, the young fish might move farther inland, toward fresh water. Over time they grew strong enough to fight the current and move upstream on their own. Some turned south at the Richelieu River, clambered up the rapids in Chambly, and reached Lake Champlain. Once in Champlain they would spend perhaps the next twenty years eating and growing before some mysterious urge pulled them back to the Atlantic Ocean. It is thought that they then returned to the Sargasso Sea to reproduce and start the cycle again, though truthfully no one really knows what happens to the adults once they reach the ocean.

For the portion of their life spent in Lake Champlain, eels tend to be found in weedy shallow waters and are most active at night. A population survey conducted in Converse, Keeler, and Paradise bays in the early 1980s estimated between 573 and 1,572 eels per acre of suitable habitat. The animals did not seem to defend small areas but rather ranged through the bays, and perhaps beyond. The eels became substantially harder to find in mid to late autumn, the time when adults began their migration to the ocean.

The voyage between ocean and inland has become more challenging for eels and other fish. Dams probably create the greatest threat. They are barriers to upstream movement, and the turbines in these dams can fillet animals moving downstream. In St-Ours and Chambly on the Richelieu River in Quebec, special devices that allow the eels to bypass the dams were installed in 1997.

Eels have also been a target of commercial fishing. The Richelieu supported a fishery until the province of Quebec suspended it in 1998. An average of almost thirty-five tons of eels was taken from the river each year. For a short time Vermont also had a commercial fishery. Commercial capture of eels on Lake Champlain began in the 1980s but was made illegal in 2002.

In recent years, fisheries biologists have noticed a marked decline in the number of eels returning to fresh water each year. Though the decline has been quite apparent in the upper St. Lawrence River system, including Lakes Champlain and Ontario, it has not been restricted to these areas. As a result, the Atlantic States Marine Fisheries Commission asked that the eel be given protection under the Endangered Species Act, a proposal the U.S. Fish and Wildlife Department is considering. Also, in May 2006 Quebec released one million young eels in the Richelieu River in an attempt to reestablish an eel population in Lake Champlain.

Of course, eels do not exist in isolation. Their population decline creates opportunities for other creatures, including those that compete with the eels and those the eels might eat. Eels are opportunistic predators of bottom-dwelling organisms. Might eels have been predators of larval sea lamprey that live in stream bottoms throughout the Champlain basin? Both field and aquarium studies have suggested the possibility. An investigation of eel diets in the Delaware River found they ate mostly insects and to a lesser degree fish, including lamprey. Only the bigger eels ate fish; however, northern eels like those in Lake Champlain tend to be larger than eels from waterways farther south.

As autumn gives way to the black-and-white landscape of winter, the eels make their way from the Gulf of St. Lawrence to warmer waters. Those still behind in the fresh water of Lake Champlain likely burrow into the mud of the lake bottom or its rivers, not yet large enough or fit enough for the arduous journey. With luck, enough of their offspring will return to protect this fascinating creature's place in Lake Champlain's ecosystem. For with their numbers dwindling, maintaining a healthy population is like holding an eel by the tail.

○ Mishe-Nahma, King of Fishes

On the white sand of the bottom
Lay the monster Mishe-Nahma,
Lay the sturgeon, King of Fishes;

In days long past, spring would bear witness to monstrous lake sturgeon (*Acipenser fulvescens*) making their way to spawning grounds along island shores and in the major tributaries of Lake Champlain. Mature fish averaged three to five feet in length, but specimens greater than seven feet long and over 300 pounds have been documented. Slow to mature, sturgeon females don't begin to reproduce until at least age fourteen, and males around age eight. Even then, females spawn only every four to nine years. Nonetheless, in 1842 naturalist Zadock Thompson described the fish as being "quite common" in Lake Champlain. Today, they are legally protected under endangered species laws in both New York and Vermont.

With his fins he fanned and winnowed,
With his tail he swept the sand-floor.

Sturgeon are wonderfully adapted for bottom feeding. The lower lobe of their tail fin is shorter than the upper so that they can hover just above the lake bottom and wave it back and forth, stirring up muck. Four whiskerlike barbels extend beneath the chin and are used to detect prey items in the sediments by both touch and taste. The entire mouth can be thrust outward to act as a vacuum, slurping up food. Sturgeon are indiscriminate feeders, taking crayfish, worms, insect larvae, leeches, other fish, and whatever else happens to be available. Presumably, when sturgeon were more numerous in Lake Champlain, they could have fed on the now abundant larvae of sea lamprey, at least in deltas.

There he lay in all his armor;
On each side a shield to guard him,

As if its great size were not sufficient to protect the fish, sturgeon sport modified hardened scales, or scutes. Two rows of scutes shield each side of the fish, while a fifth row covers its back. Each scute hosts a sharp spine, though the spines wear down over time and may not be visible in older individuals. Sturgeon scutes were responsible for shredding numerous fishing nets in early America. At the same time, early Americans had no use for the meat of the sturgeon. Thompson offered qualified praise, saying "Its flesh, though not generally very much esteemed, if properly cooked is very good eating." Due to the damage it inflicted on gear and its own inutility, sturgeon were much despised through much of American history. Caught fish were heaved on shore and burned or simply left to rot.

"Take my bait, O Sturgeon, Nahma!
Come up from below the water,
Let us see which is the stronger!"

In the late 1800s the appeal of the sturgeon changed dramatically, as documented by Richard Adams Carey in his book *The Philosopher Fish*. Eastern European immigrants, who had eaten sturgeon in their home countries, lacked the biases of earlier settlers. They also discovered that America's sturgeon could produce caviar comparable in quality to that of the Caspian Sea. A commercial market quickly developed, focused principally on Atlantic sturgeon, but also exploiting the lake sturgeon. In addition to the fish's meat and caviar, part of the sturgeon's swim bladder was marketed as isinglass and used as a clarifying agent in wine and beer.

And again the sturgeon, Nahma,
Gasped and quivered in the water,
Then was still, and drifted landward

It didn't take long for the resource to be overexploited. According to Carey, "In little more than two decades, the eternal sturgeon had gone the way of the buffalo, the passenger pigeon, and the Atlantic salmon. But since caviar itself had never become part of the mainstream American diet, remaining instead a food largely for immigrants, foreigners, or bigwigs, the sturgeon disappeared with none of those other animals' tragic fanfare." The development of commercial markets was one more strike against the species after the profligate waste of earlier days and the loss of spawning habitat following the damming of most major rivers.

Till the waves washed through the rib-bones,
Till the sea-gulls came no longer,
And upon the sands lay nothing
But the skeleton of Nahma.

The fate of Lake Champlain's sturgeon is not yet as dire as that of Henry Wadsworth Longfellow's Mishe-Nahma from the *Song of Hiawatha*. Some fish still cruise the depths. In 2004 the Vermont Fish & Wildlife Department reported that it had found naturally produced sturgeon eggs in the Winooski, Lamoille, and Missisquoi rivers. A larval sturgeon was also captured in Otter Creek. The results were pleasantly surprising, especially since attempts to find adults for study resulted in the capture of only male fish. New York has begun a lake sturgeon stocking program, though initial efforts are not focused on Lake Champlain. With luck, patience, and careful stewardship, perhaps future springs will once again see masses of sturgeon spawning in the Lake Champlain basin.

⭕ Degrees of Separation

Social theory suggests that any two people in the world can be connected by only a few degrees of separation. So, for example, if my sister's coworker knows your aunt's bridge partner's babysitter, we are separated by six degrees. The idea, also called the "small-world hypothesis," was first proposed in the 1960s but became particularly popular after the play and movie *Six Degrees of Separation* were released in the early 1990s. The concept even spawned a game whereby participants tried to link the actor Kevin Bacon to any other actor through their movies using at most six links. While considering the degrees of separation between people leads to interesting parlor games, considering degrees of separation between species can reveal some surprising ecological effects.

Charles Darwin speculated about such species interactions as far back as 1859 when he described a possible ecological connection between house cats and flowers, mediated by three degrees of separation. Certain flowers depend upon bees for pollination. Bee nests were found to be more numerous near villages than in the countryside. Many bee nests are destroyed by mice. Fewer mice are found near villages than in the countryside because of predation of house cats. Thus house cats, through interactions with mice that interact with bees, can improve the ability of flowers to produce seeds.

Such diffuse interactions occur in aquatic as well as terrestrial systems. For example, zebra mussels are thought to clear the way for invasion from other exotic species. Round goby, a fish species from Eastern Europe, found a familiar food source—zebra mussels—when they came to the Great Lakes after the zebra mussels. More locally, zebra mussels' filter feeding has increased the clarity of the water column in Lake Champlain, allowing plants to grow to a greater depth and thus colonize more of the lake.

Much research on diffuse aquatic interactions has focused on the role of predators in controlling algae blooms and vice versa. It seems that an absence of predators can promote algae blooms through three degrees of separation. Without predators, small fish that eat plankton thrive, and the plankton that would otherwise eat algae decline.

The greatest challenge to the small-world hypothesis comes from insulated tribes, much like those that have been found in the Amazon jungles. Yet with just a few interactions with the outside world, such islands mix in with the network of social connections.

Lakes themselves are among the more insulated components of ecological systems. They are linked to other bodies of water via river networks that are quite different ecologically from lakes. And clearly a lake is separated from the terrestrial world around it. Yet species interactions have been shown to cross even these seemingly difficult ecological barriers.

In the Northwest, bears transfer nutrients from aquatic systems to uplands when they remove large numbers of spawning salmon from the water. This leads to increased growth of vegetation in riparian forests, according to research from the University of Washington.

Species still living in the water can also influence the terrestrial landscape, as demonstrated by researchers at Washington University in St. Louis and the University of Florida. They observed that the presence or absence of fish in a pond could affect the pollination of nearby flowers, with no fish meaning less pollination. How could this be? The answer involved predation and dragonflies. Dragonflies spend the first part of their life as aquatic larvae, vulnerable to fish predation. Once dragonflies become the aerial predators with which we are more familiar, they feed heavily on potential flower pollinators. Lots of fish means fewer dragonflies and thus more pollinators. Without fish, more dragonflies hatch, and the pollinator population decreases. Thus fish, through three degrees of separation, can influence the pollination of flowers.

In another example, the round gobies that followed zebra mussels into the Great Lakes may have a negative impact on birds, though this relationship is not yet proven. The gobies eat mussels containing a bacterium that causes avian botulism. The gobies are affected by the botulism but survive in a weakened state for a period of time, during which they become more susceptible to predation from fish-eating birds, which contract the bacteria. Since 2000, tens of thousands of loons, gulls, and diving ducks have been found dead on the shores of Lakes Erie and Ontario after having succumbed to botulism.

John Muir, the famed naturalist and writer, once noted, "When we try to pick out anything by itself, we find it hitched to everything else in the universe." Sometimes the hitch is obvious, like cats and mice, but sometimes it's more subtle, like fish and flowers. With just a few degrees of separation, the fundamental truth of Muir's observation can be demonstrated again and again. To understand an ecosystem, we need to pay attention not just to the most popular game fish and their largest prey, but to the little things as well.

○ Mini-Monsters, Little Wheels, Oar Feet, and Prongs

Size is not a meaningful indication of importance in an ecosystem, as consideration of some of Lake Champlain's tiniest animals should demonstrate.

Among the lake's smaller denizens, one seems particularly monsterlike. It undertakes nightly ascents of the water column, seemingly in pursuit of the moon. Large eyes bulge out on stalks above its head. Its six legs propel it speedily toward prey above. Four additional arms strain the water before them, removing anything remotely resembling food and sweeping it toward smaller appendages that hold the food before the creature's crushing jaws. Onward the monster comes, straining upward until suddenly it reaches a magical barrier. If opossum shrimp, *Mysis relicta*, were not just an inch long, they might be as scary as the Creature from the Black Lagoon.

Freshwater *Mysis* by the thousands spend their days in deep, cold, nutrient-poor water, rising to feed each evening. By staying in cold water they reduce their metabolic rate and thus their need for food. Once nightfall comes, their predators have a more difficult time seeing them, so *Mysis* can feed more safely. However, *Mysis* can't tolerate water warmer than about 50 degrees Fahrenheit, because at higher temperatures their metabolic rate increases so much that they process and excrete food faster than they can ingest it—thus the "magical barrier" of warm water.

Mysis are among the most important food sources for lake trout and forage fish like rainbow smelt. Additionally, their daily vertical migrations serve to transfer nutrients and energy from sediment and deeper water up into the water column. Typically, nutrients and energy enter the lake's food web when they are captured by plankton near the water surface. As these organisms die, their bodies and all that they had accumulated in life fall to the lake bottom. There they would stay if it weren't for the daily vertical migrations of *Mysis*.

But when *Mysis* travel up the water column, they bring more than just food and energy with them. Hidden in the lake's sediment are accumulations of PCBs and mercury from decades of deposition. Since *Mysis* spend half their life in close contact with sediments, they accumulate the toxics and transfer them up the food chain as well.

Worldwide there are over 1,000 species of *Mysis*, mostly from marine environments; there are only three freshwater species in the United States. Their common name, opossum shrimp, comes from their trait of carrying young in a pouch beneath their belly. Lake Champlain is part of their natural range, which stretches east and north from the Great Plains, through the Great Lakes, into Canada and across to Eurasia.

In addition to these native populations, *Mysis* have often been introduced to western lakes, ostensibly to improve the sport fishery, though the actual consequences turned out somewhat differently. The *Mysis* were expected to provide forage for native salmon and trout but instead caused declines in these species. Native species that rely heavily on visual foraging, such as kokanee salmon and cutthroat trout, were ill-prepared to take advantage of the *Mysis* with their nightly vertical migrations. Additionally, the *Mysis* competed with juvenile salmon for the same plankton food sources. Meanwhile, lake trout and whitefish (which were also frequently introduced to western lakes) were accustomed to feeding in low light conditions, and they thrived, providing further competition for the native species.

Ecological effects extended beyond the lake where the introductions occurred. As the salmon population declined following the *Mysis* introduction to Flathead Lake in Montana, one study documented a concurrent decline in eagle and bear populations due to a reduction in their food. *Mysis*, so crucial to lakes where they are native, including Champlain, really can be as scary as movie monsters in western lakes where they are introduced.

The other three of our organisms are microscopic or nearly so; the very largest reach only about a tenth of an inch in length. Because of their small size, they have little ability to regulate their position in the water column as *Mysis* do. Rather, they float with waves and currents. These three could be called little wheels, oar feet, and prongs—literal translations of their descriptive scientific names of rotifers, copepods, and cladocera. They constitute the three most common groups of zooplankton, animals that float about in the middle of the lake, drifting where wind and currents take them, with limited ability to propel themselves.

Rotifers are the most distinct of the group. Unlike copepods and cladocerans (which are at least distantly related to somewhat more familiar animals like shrimp), rotifers inhabit a group unto themselves. In body shape they resemble an urn, wide-based with a slight constriction near the top, and then a wider mouth area. Around the outside of the mouth, short hairs constantly wave. The coordinated movement of the hairs makes them appear like two small whirling wheels and gives rotifers their name. Rotifers are the smallest of the three zooplankton groups, typically one-quarter to one-half the size of cladocerans or copepods. They eat any organic particles they can ingest and are in turn eaten by a number of organisms larger than they are.

Females dominate in rotifer populations; in fact, males are unknown for most species. However, those species that do have males have two different kinds of females. The most common type of female lays "summer eggs" that do not require fertilization and hatch to be more females. The second type of female lays a different egg that may follow one of two paths. If this egg is fertilized by a male, it produces a thick-walled cell called a "winter egg" that can lie dormant for months or years. If it is not fertilized, this egg can hatch and become a male.

Copepods—our oar feet—resemble scorpions in body shape, minus the claws and stingers. But instead of scuttling like scorpions do, their legs hang below their bodies and beat in rhythm, like scullers in a skiff, to provide some mobility.

Two principal groups of copepods live in the lake—cyclopoids and calanoids. Calanoids filter their food, while cyclopoids, the dominant form, more actively hunt. Like the one-eyed giant of Greek myth, cyclopoids have a single spot, sensitive to light, in the midst of their "head."

Typical cladocerans—our prongs—resemble overweight ghosts. What appears to be an angular bowed head sits atop a rotund body with no visible legs, while long-fingered hands extend in a threatening pose. What appear to be arms are actually antennae—the "prongs" that give the group its name. Actual appendages are small, not jutting from the body, and highly modified for feeding. Like most zooplankton, cladocerans feed on anything floating in the water that fits in their mouth, including algae, bacteria, and smaller zooplankton. In turn, cladocerans are the principal food source for many small fish, constituting up to 95 percent of stomach content volume in some studies, and rarely less than 10 percent.

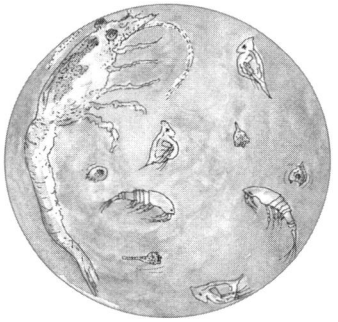

Most cladocerans are female, and in many species males are unknown. In those species with males, the males appear only in the autumn or spring. In those species without males, females lay unfertilized eggs capable of developing into full adults.

The first study of zooplankton in Lake Champlain took place in 1929. Populations of the three groups differ among different lake segments. While copepods are more numerous in the Main Lake, cladocerans dominate in other areas. Rotifers exceed the other two types in number, but because of their small size they are fewer by weight.

Between 1929 and about 1994, no significant changes in zooplankton populations were recorded by the various individuals studying the community. After that, Tim Mihuc and his graduate assistant from the State University of New York at Plattsburgh detected a substantial decline in rotifers. Whereas rotifers had constituted about 80 percent of the number of individuals in the early 1990s, by 1994 they accounted for less than 40 percent and in some sites as little as 5 percent, and there was a decline in the number of species found. Meanwhile, the number of copepod species increased.

Exact reasons for the change in species composition are unknown. However, the authors do note that the timing corresponds with the arrival of zebra mussels in the lake. On the other hand, changes in zooplankton populations happened nearly simultaneously throughout the lake, while zebra mussels moved north only slowly, over a period of about ten years.

A dramatic change in the wildlife community of Lake Champlain had occurred, yet there were no press reports, no calls for action—in fact, not even a clear idea of what it meant for the lake as a whole. It is inevitable; small animals escape attention. Perhaps they may herald larger changes yet to come in the lake, or maybe the change is but one more consequence of what has already been done.

○ Home for the Holidays

Planes, trains, and automobiles: humans have a variety of means for hopscotching the country as they travel hither and yon for the holiday season. Aquatic animals lack any such contrivances. Yet, if you were to dig a new upland pond, it would soon become filled with all sorts of wiggly microscopic creatures. How do seemingly immobile creatures traverse the inhospitable terrain between the nearest lake and a new home?

The relatives who live nearby and can drive are most likely to put in an appearance at the holiday party. Similarly, organisms that can move themselves like mammals and insects spread most easily. They simply fly or walk from one habitat to another. Those wiggling mosquito larvae that end up in spring pools were deposited as eggs by a flying adult. Even some slow-moving organisms like aquatic snails or some flightless beetles have been documented crawling over land of their own volition.

Does every family have at least one relative who just never seems to get home for the celebrations? Within a species, some individuals may be more or less adept at dispersing. For example, water strider and water beetle species have long-winged and short-winged individuals within a population. Typically, the short-winged forms produce many more babies than long-winged forms, but long-winged forms are better at dispersing. So the long-wings can find new habitats when the old ponds dry up or otherwise become less favorable, while the short wings just stay put.

Everyone's sympathies go out to the poor college student on the opposite side of the country with no car and no family nearby, but on occasion even he or she manages to get back home. Many organisms have no way of moving themselves, yet they are still capable of colonizing new habitats. These critters must depend on some other medium—physical or biological—to convey them from one place to another.

Physical means of transport might include wind and water. Small artificial pools constructed near a known source of animals will be colonized even if all organisms larger than one millimeter are prevented from accessing the water. In these cases, wind transport of organisms is presumed, in part due to lack of evidence for any other mechanism. Water transport is best known from streams, where larval insects that live under rocks might drift slowly downstream throughout their life. Both mechanisms sound easier than fighting the crowds and delayed flights at airports around holidays.

Some organisms even hitchhike. Larval water mites can attach to flying insects for a free ride. In some cases, the in-flight beverage includes the blood of the host, as the mites may be parasitic. Juvenile zebra mussels have been found attached to duck feathers. Bryozoans, small colonial animals that resemble corals, can form two different types of reproductive buds: when population densities are low, they form a smooth type, and when population densities are high, they form a type with little hooks that presumably attach to passing water birds and allow the offspring to move to less-crowded habitats. Hitchhikers can even travel inside of animals. Eggs of various organisms can still hatch after passing through the guts of waterfowl, fish, or even mammals like muskrats.

Of course, humans frequently provide a ride to aquatic hitchhikers. Hitchhikers might attach to clothing, fishing tackle, or bait buckets, but likely the most prominent vector is boats. For one nonnative water flea in the Midwest, a study found, "nonhuman dispersal mechanisms play an insignificant role in range expansion"—which is another way of saying that people likely provided the ride.

While family celebrations offer a welcome opportunity for fellowship, reminiscing, and love, many are also marred by stress, bickering, and those particularly annoying relatives. Similarly, the ability of small organisms to hopscotch long distances over inhospitable terrain to colonize new water bodies has both good points and bad. On the plus side, colonization allows gene flow between isolated water bodies. As our climate warms, this provides a way for organisms to spread naturally to habitats that become more welcoming. Colonization allowed lakes to fill with life after the glaciers departed the landscape, and it allows a species to persist even if the water body in which it evolved fills in over geologic time. On the downside, nonnative species, like the fishhook water flea and spiny water flea, that have caused changes in food webs of the Great Lakes, could travel to Lake Champlain by means over which we have absolutely no control.

Animals may lack vehicles, but they still find an astounding array of travel options. And they take advantage of them even without the promise of a home-cooked meal at the other end.

○ Striding over the Water

My wife and I were enjoying a canoe outing when our fourteen-month-old daughter suddenly decided she wanted to play with the "bugs" on the water surface. With some effort we were able to keep her from climbing over the side, but she just did not understand why she, too, couldn't scoot around on top of the water. As I thought about it, what I couldn't understand was why the insects could move about so freely without fear of sinking.

Water striders, whirligig beetles, and fishing spiders take advantage of an intriguing property of water—its surface tension. The molecules at the surface of the water are like an insular cult: hesitant to accept newcomers and resistant to letting go of their own members. Each molecule has a strong attraction to the molecules next to or below it. There is no corresponding attraction to anything above. As a result, a tense film exists at the interface between water and air, which can prevent objects from sinking. The surface tension allows foam and spring pollen to float.

While tension prevents the critters from slipping between water molecules, staying on top of the film requires them also to displace a volume of water that weighs more than they do. Objects placed on top of the water exert a pressure downward based upon the volume of water they displace. The water pushes back up with a force equal to the mass of that displaced volume. As long as the downward pressure is not greater than the upward pressure, the object floats. The sum of pressures is referred to as buoyancy.

To help increase the amount of water they displace, some creatures secrete waxes and other compounds that repel water. The compounds coat the legs of the "bugs" and create dimples in the water surface around each leg. In addition to pushing more water away, the dimples change the orientation of some of the water molecules at the surface. Those molecules on the walls of the dimples start applying pressure upward, giving the dimples a springlike quality that also helps the creature float.

There is, however, a problem created by having waxy stuff on your legs: how can you move? Movement requires pushing against or pulling toward some relatively stagnant force. When we walk we push against the earth; when a jet plane flies it simultaneously pulls against the air in front of it and pushes against the air behind it. Since water molecules are repelled from the tips of the animals' legs, when the "bugs" wave their legs across the surface there is limited counterpressure. To them it is like constantly standing on super-slippery ice. Dr. Robert Suter at Vassar College has spent a good deal of time trying to understand how critters can move in such an environment. His work focuses on fishing spiders. (Presumably water striders use the same mechanism, but whirligig beetles may have a different means of locomotion.)

Fishing spiders move principally by rowing. The legs of the spiders act like the shafts of paddles, while the dimples themselves act as blades. Dimples create enough drag in the water that the spider can push against them. When the dimple is pushed back, a vacuum is created in front of it. Water rushes to fill the vacuum, and the spider moves forward on the current created.

Rowing has limitations, though. When they row, spiders use only their middle two pairs of legs. The front and back pairs rest on the surface of the water to stabilize the spiders and help them steer. In the bigger species, the body also rests on the water. All these extra points of contact create resistance to each stroke. It is like trying to bicycle with the brakes on; the spider does not glide at all and has to work pretty hard to move a short distance. Additionally, if the spider pushes its legs down too hard or too fast, it can break the dimple, which is like paddling with just a pole and no blade. Suter has found that these factors limit how fast the spiders can row, and it is not fast enough to escape potential predators.

When a spider really has to boogie, it gallops. In galloping the spider lifts all eight legs and its body off the surface of the water with each stride. Thus there is no resistance from the water, only from less viscous air, resulting in a more efficient coasting period between strides. During galloping, the spider uses three pairs of legs for propulsion rather than the two pairs used during rowing. Upon returning to the water the legs will break into the water surface temporarily, and the horizontal force of the water pushing against the legs shoots the spider into the air. It is like forcing a pen cap underwater and then letting go, at which the cap rockets up.

When the spider is surprised, it can use a similar strategy to execute an amazing standing leap. The spider slams all eight legs into the water and shoots up over an inch and a half. Relative to the spider's size that is about equivalent to a six-foot basketball player jumping onto the roof of a two-story house from a standing start, in newly poured concrete! The spider just hopes it's enough to avoid a fish slurping up treats from the water's surface.

For real long-distance travel, the spider has yet another means of moving about. The animal merely lifts its body and a few legs off the water and lets the wind push it along—a technique that should sound familiar to sailors.

Anyone who has taken the time to glide quietly over placid water can begin to appreciate that here is a different world. In order to make a living in this world, insects and spiders have developed amazing adaptations, worthy of attention. I hope my daughter maintains her fascination with these creatures. I look forward to her suggesting more questions about them.

◯ Is a Mussel a Mussel?

Is a blue jay a duck? That question was posed to a graduate-level class I once took. The answer of course is "yes": if one is trying to understand the impacts of a pollutant on birds, or trying to understand how birds differ from other organisms, then a blue jay is indeed the same as a duck, since both are birds. Or the answer is "no," if the subject of study is different types of birds. The ludicrous question seems less silly when applied to more cryptic organisms. For example, is a mussel a mussel?

Nearly 300 different species of freshwater mussels inhabit North America, according to the U.S. Fish and Wildlife Service; that is the highest diversity of freshwater mussels in the world. Most of that diversity is centered in the Midwest, but Lake Champlain and its basin host sixteen different species, more than in all of Europe.

In the taxonomic scheme used to classify organisms, birds are lumped in the same class. Within that class are many orders, including one for ducks and one for all perching birds, including blue jays, sparrows, and warblers. Within each order are different families, which can then be subdivided into different genera, and each of these genera might contain multiple species. There are about 10,000 species of birds.

Comparatively, mussels share the bivalve class with clams, scallops, and oysters, all of which are aquatic, have two shells covering their body, and have a large muscu-

lar hatchet-shaped foot. There are about 15,000 species of bivalves, the vast majority found in the ocean. Most of Lake Champlain's mussel species are found in a single family, which means they are taxonomically more similar to one another than a blue jay is to a duck, but about as alike as a blue jay is to a crow.

Can mussels really be even as different from one another as a blue jay and a crow? Birds offer some resemblance to us in the way they are put together. Certainly they differ in having wings and feathers, but we recognize their eyes and legs, so we can study familiar features and detect differences in color, body shape, beak shape, voice, and so on, to distinguish species. Even with something as odd as a snail we can at least tell the front from the back. What is there about a mussel to help us pick out different species? They have no head, and most of their body consists of a single large foot.

Paul Marangelo, an ecologist with the Nature Conservancy, has some experience answering that question. I spent a day with him on the Poultney River surveying mussel species. We found six species, some obviously distinct. The pink heelsplitter has an inch-high triangular projection on the back of its shell. Imagine a careless foot falling onto that shell, and you realize how the species earned its name. The pocketbook has a thick shell and a much more rounded shape than other species. Still other species remained enigmatic even after the day's work.

Where the mussels really differ from one another is in their reproductive biology. Freshwater mussels release larvae called glochidia that hitchhike on fish or sometimes amphibians. The means by which the parent releases glochidia and the specific host for the larvae differ from species to species. Some species, like the pocketbook, lure the future host in close. They dangle a piece of tissue outside their shell that resembles a small fish. When a larger fish swims over to investigate, the pocketbook spits out a mass of larvae.

Probably the greatest threat to native mussels in Lake Champlain has been the arrival of the infamous zebra mussel from Europe. Since their discovery in 1993, zebra mussels have come to dominate much of the near-shore lake bottom. They clog water intake pipes, slice the feet of swimmers, coat historic shipwrecks, and smother native mussels.

Zebra mussels are of a lineage very different from that of North American species. If native mussels are blue jays and crows, zebra mussels are ducks, or maybe even ostriches. Instead of attaching to passing fish, zebra mussel larvae float freely in the water column. This reproductive strategy makes them more similar to their marine relatives than are the other freshwater mussels.

To date, zebra mussels have failed to move far upstream from the lake. Perhaps the free-floating larvae are unable to migrate against river currents. Thus, the bottomland rivers like the Poultney provide a refuge for the native species. These areas are where one can best determine the differences between mussels and mussels.

◯ A Long Winter's Nap

I used to envy the life of turtles. Their hard shells protect them from most predators. No one expects them to move very quickly. And best of all, they get to spend all summer swimming around the lake and all winter sleeping. However, as idyllic and restful as a turtle's winter might sound, hibernation is no easy task.

Two of winter's big challenges are cold and lack of food. As temperatures fall below the freezing point, water in living cells turns to ice. Since ice is less dense than cold water, it also expands and may rupture cell walls. Humans know the condition as frostbite. Food is unavailable largely because plants and insects, two prime food sources, react to the cold by entering their own states of dormancy. With some notable exceptions, most

Map turtle in Windmill Bay (photo by Megan Epler Wood)

animals that have not built up a reserve of fat or stashed a winter's supply of food do not survive.

Animals employ three general strategies to cope with winter's challenges. Many birds, some humans, and a few insects like monarch butterflies migrate to warmer climates. The migrations require tremendous amounts of energy, and once the migrants arrive on the wintering grounds, they must deal with competition from local residents and a multitude of parasites not found on their breeding grounds. Other birds and most mammals stick around and try to weather the season. Their challenge is finding enough food to maintain high internal body temperatures. The third strategy, and the one employed by most turtles, is to enter a prolonged period of dormancy and reduced metabolic activity, and thus avoid the need for large quantities of food. The challenge to these hibernators is to avoid (or in some cases tolerate) freezing.

Hibernators seek out areas insulated from the bitterest cold of winter to avoid freezing. Bats head to caves where the average temperature is constant year-round. Chipmunks burrow underground where the combination of the earth and the snowpack provides insulation. Turtles stay under the ice cover of rivers, lakes, or ponds where temperatures remain constant through the winter; but living underwater presents a separate challenge.

The ice that protects deep water from freezing also prevents any oxygen from diffusing into the system, yet many creatures living underwater—fish, invertebrates, and others besides turtles—still need it. At the bottom of the lake, a host of mud-dwelling decomposers quickly uses up the oxygen while recycling the year's detritus, making conditions even more challenging. The inactivity of hibernation reduces, but does not eliminate, the need for oxygen. Even those turtle species most tolerant of low oxygen conditions seek springs or inlets that keep concentrations somewhat higher.

To make matters worse for turtles, they have lungs; most animals that live below the water for extended periods use gills for breathing instead. Water flows across the gills, rather than in and out, as air flows in lungs. As anyone who has swallowed a mouthful of water while swimming knows, it is pretty difficult to move water in and out of lungs. Water has a much lower concentration of oxygen than air, even when holding all the oxygen it possibly can. Lungs are not nearly as efficient at extracting oxygen from water as gills are. Even though fish have gills, hard winters kill many of them if the oxygen under the ice becomes depleted. Many a March following a hard winter I have watched eagles and gulls feasting on piles of dead carp at Dead Creek in Addison, Vermont.

Turtles manage to tolerate low oxygen concentrations by breathing through their skin. In particular, they absorb oxygen through the lining of the mouth, the legs, and the cloaca (roughly equivalent to an anus), with uptake being most efficient through the lining of the mouth. Species that rely exclusively on skin breathing to survive the winter, like map and spiny soft-shell turtles, must hibernate in areas where oxygen is available in the water throughout the season.

A secondary strategy, used by painted and snapping turtles, is to switch in part to chemical pathways that don't require oxygen. Humans also adopt this strategy for limited periods when engaged in strenuous exercise. The alternative pathways are less efficient and create yet another problem. While respiration with oxygen produces carbon dioxide, a relatively harmless gas, as a waste product, alternate pathways produce acids. Buildup of acids in muscle tissue causes the familiar aches and stiffness we feel after a day of exercise. Imagine building up those acids over months of hibernation.

Painted turtles counter the buildup of acids by liberating calcium carbonate from their shells. The calcium carbonate acts like an antacid tablet and neutralizes the acids, preventing them from accumulating in the blood and muscles. Calcium makes turtle shells strong, just as it does bones and teeth. It may be that soft-shell turtles cannot utilize this strategy because they have less calcium in their shells.

A January thaw can provide a respite for animals hibernating on land, a chance to awaken and replenish diminished stores of fat. Under the water there is no respite until the spring thaw. Oxygen continues to be depleted, with no replenishment, while painted and snapping turtles continue to mobilize calcium reserves in their shells to buffer acids. Winter becomes a marathon endurance trial, and only the hardiest survive it. The idyllic life of a turtle seems less enviable to me now.

6

THE FUTURE OF LAKE CHAMPLAIN

Attempting to understand the future of Lake Champlain requires an acknowledgment of relevant time scales at which change can occur. Landscape changes accelerated greatly following the arrival of Europeans. By the early 1800s a substantial portion of the forested landscape that Samuel de Champlain saw when he traversed the lake in 1609 had been converted to farmland. Since the 1830s much of that farmland has regenerated to forest. And now houses and shopping malls are an integral component of the landscape. Colonization of the lake by new species was extremely rapid following the retreat of the glaciers. More recently, it has been humans who have been responsible for moving numerous species between water bodies, both purposefully and inadvertently. The lake does not reflect today's actions so much as yesterday's.

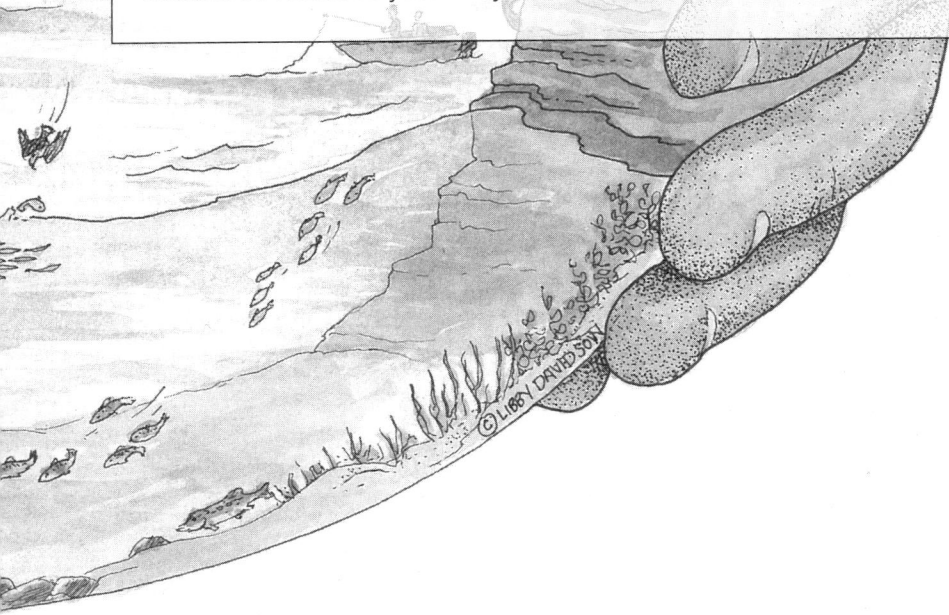

◯ Periodic Events and Predictability

Periodic, dramatic changes at unanticipated intervals complicate predictions about the future of Lake Champlain and often have greater ecological impacts than do slow, steady pressures. Change in nature does not proceed linearly. As a result, our ability to understand any ecological event or process is affected by the time scale through which it is viewed. Typically, we focus only on at most one human lifetime or more likely just a few decades, thus missing or misunderstanding events that occur less frequently.

Imagine trying to understand Lake Champlain without ever considering the effects of winter. Winter ushers in a predictable series of events with which organisms must cope. The waters of the lake become uniform in temperature and mix from top to bottom. Then, as temperatures fall further, the surface of the lake solidifies to ice, reducing the amount of sunlight than can penetrate and preventing diffusion of oxygen into the water until the thaw. Humans, with our decades-long life spans, experience many winters in our days, and thus we have learned the importance of storing food and stocking fuel to keep us warm; but even organisms with life spans of only days or weeks have evolved to adapt to winter. Thus algae produce cells that go dormant for months, and annual plants produce seeds that can withstand freezing.

On an even smaller time scale, consider the differences in the lake between day and night. Certain species, like opossum shrimp, migrate upward in the lake at night, both to feed and to avoid being fed upon by daytime predators. Other species, like blue-green algae, instead move downward at night and migrate upward during the day, to take advantage of light for photosynthesis.

For humans, it is much more difficult to adapt to events that occur irregularly over large time scales. Devastating weather events like hurricanes or ice storms are an example. The return time for major hurricanes (winds greater than 111 miles per hour) hitting southern New York is estimated at eighty years, and the last one struck in 1938. Ecological effects of that storm can still be found by careful observers. And broken branches and snapped tree crowns from the 1998 ice storm are still visible in many areas of the Champlain Valley

Periods of severe storminess have recurred fairly regularly in the Northeast. Researchers at the University of Vermont examined sediment cores in lakes throughout the region and detected periods of intense sedimentation, probably resulting from a series of massive storms. These stormy periods recur on average every 3,000 years and last for up to 1,500 years. Such natural variability in storminess at a time scale far beyond what an individual human can experience makes it difficult to distinguish natural changes from human-induced impacts on climate.

○ Lag Times

Just as episodic events help us understand the present, lag times help us understand the response of the lake to changes. Lag times can be found throughout our lives. Digital cameras often have a lag between the moment the shutter-release button is depressed and when the image is recorded, making it difficult to capture fast-paced, one-time events. There is a lag between when I send my tax return to the IRS and actually get a refund. There is a lag between when I take an aspirin and when my headache disappears. There is a lag between when I foolishly bushwhack through poison ivy and when I awake covered with oozing rashes. Lake Champlain experiences significant lag times, too.

One of the most reliable lag times occurs following rainstorms. Major rivers swell with floodwaters only a day or two after the storms that unleash the extra water. The rainwater takes time to infiltrate through soil and make its way downstream, and the farther downstream, the greater the lag time. In heavily urbanized areas, the lag time is reduced because roads, buildings, and parking lots shed water much faster than forests and fields. Thus, peak flows in urban streams come close on the heels of storms and carry a larger portion of the storm flow at one time.

Lag times also occur in association with the three big threats to Lake Champlain: invasive species, toxics, and nutrient pollution.

There is often a lag between when an invasive species first appears in the lake and when it becomes established. Zebra mussels offer the clearest example. They were first found in the South Lake in 1993 and in three years had spread through the Main Lake, yet adults were only confirmed in Missisquoi Bay twelve years later, in 2005.

With toxics, there is a lag time between addressing the source of the problem and seeing beneficial effects in the lake. PCBs have been a toxic pollutant of concern for many years. Manufacturing of PCBs was banned in 1979, and the chemicals were dredged from Cumberland Bay by 2001. Sediment cores show dramatic reductions in PCB concentrations since then. Nonetheless, both Vermont and New York still caution anglers against eating certain types of fish because of high PCB concentrations. There is a substantial lag between reducing the inputs of these pollutants to the lake and reducing concentrations in fish flesh. Beyond that, there is a lag between the time concentrations might be reduced in fish flesh and the time government policies might respond to the change.

Mercury movement through the environment provides another example of lag times. Like PCBs, mercury is a persistent toxic chemical that accumulates in fish tissue. Researchers from the Academy of Natural Sciences have suggested mercury deposited years ago may not be readily assimilated into food chains, instead becoming bound in sediment particles. It can take at least two years for mercury that falls from the sky to make its way through a drainage basin and into a lake. However, mercury that lands directly in the lake takes only about three weeks to make its way into the food chain.

Perhaps the most distressing evidence of lag times in lakes is in a lake's response to nutrient pollution-reduction efforts. Once excess nutrients enter the lake system, they can be stored in the sediment. However, when oxygen is depleted from deep water, as happens during the summer in some shallow areas, the nutrients can be remobilized. Furthermore, within streams nutrients can be stored in slugs of sediment that enter the water during flood events and slowly make their way downstream. Efforts to prevent future slugs don't address past conditions. Indeed, published research conducted at the Coweeta Long Term Ecological Research Station suggests land uses in watersheds during the 1950s better predict water quality than do present-day land uses. It may take at least decades for the system to respond to today's water-quality improvement efforts.

The duration of a lag time must be considered in comparison to the phenomenon being observed. A one-second lag time on a camera does not matter if the photographer is trying to capture a crawling snail; it is insufferably long if the subject is a diving swimmer. Long lag times associated with ecosystem responses to water-quality improvement are most troublesome if they deter those efforts. After all, election cycles, so important to politicians who provide funding for restoration work, are much shorter than the lake's lag times. It took decades of neglect to degrade water bodies; it will take decades of attention to improve them.

◯ Large-Scale Changes

Three large-scale changes relevant to the future of Lake Champlain appear to be occurring at this time. First, the landscape of the basin continues to be altered as a result of human uses. Before Europeans arrived, forests dominated. As the land was settled, it was cleared and converted to small-scale agriculture. Now many of the forests have regrown, but at the same time the scale and intensity of agricultural practices has increased, and development of the land for housing and modern life has expanded rapidly. Second, the composition of species that inhabit the lake has changed and continues to change. At first the change was in the direction of loss, as overexploitation and deterioration of spawning habitat led to extirpation of many species, such as lake trout and salmon, and severe depletion of other species, such as lake sturgeon and American eel. Now, changes in species composition mean the accidental introduction or spread of nonnative species to the lake. Zebra mussels provide the most vivid example. Third, changes in local weather patterns resulting from global warming will likely impact the lake. Precisely how each of these three variables will affect the lake is inherently unknowable, but any attempt to understand the future of the lake must consider them.

Land Use: Urban, Suburban

Before entering Lake Champlain, Potash Brook winds through a lovely forest of hemlock and assorted other tree species. The area offers a haven for different woodpeckers and is often filled with the loud drumming of pileateds and the squeaks of hairys. Tracks of mice and fox and raccoons crisscross the forest floor. At the confluence with Lake Champlain, the brook passes through a sand delta spotted with willows. Observing the upland flora and fauna at this location, it is hard to imagine that pollution in Potash Brook made it the subject of a very public lawsuit.

Potash Brook is an impaired waterway. This relatively small brook carries excess sediment and phosphorus (which promotes algal growth) each year to Lake Champlain (one 1977 estimate suggested nutrient loads as high as 1,630 pounds per year). The lower reaches of the brook are unable to support aquatic life. In addition to sediments and phosphorus, the brook carries oil, grease, metals, and various organic compounds.

The impairment of Potash Brook is not caused by insidious, greedy industry callously discharging its waste; rather it is a victim of numerous small cuts from urban stormwater runoff. Potash Brook winds through rapidly developing South Burlington, Vermont. There are over 100 permitted and unpermitted stormwater discharges into the brook. For approximately 1.5 miles the brook runs parallel to Interstate 189 and receives stormwater discharge from this busy roadway.

Burlington waterfront (photo by Carolyn L. Bates)

Stormwater pollution is predominately a problem of urbanized areas, and urbanization in the Lake Champlain basin has been increasing. Between the 1990 and 2000 censuses, the population of the basin increased approximately 5 percent, with rates of growth in Vermont's Chittenden and Franklin counties more than twice that of the basin average. A report by the Brookings Institution has noted that in Burlington, the largest city in the basin, developed land increased at twice the rate of population growth.

The wet, stormy autumn of my first year in graduate school provided my introduction to the issue of stormwater. Prior to that I had been working outside in the woods in all sorts of weather. Through the many storms I was struck by the quantity of water that poured down the streets and along curbs—it was a phenomenon I had never noticed in the country. At first I attributed the water to the steepness of the hill in downtown Burlington and the ability of the streets to acts as chutes. However, when my wife noticed the runoff, she challenged my explanation, and it didn't hold up very well. "Isn't the area where you worked steeper than the Burlington hill?" she asked. Well, yes, quite a bit steeper. "Weren't there channels and gullies there that didn't fill with water after every rain? Why didn't they act as chutes?" My explanation quickly fell apart.

What really differed about the landscape in Burlington was that soil had been replaced by impervious surfaces. A bird's-eye view of an urban or suburban landscape reveals rooftops, parking lots, driveways, and roads. Where the soil had acted as a sponge to absorb rainwater and then dribble it out slowly over time, impervious surfaces act like a coating of aluminum foil over the sponge, sloughing off the water immediately. Once between 10 and 20 percent of a landscape is impervious, surfaces become connected and water can channel directly to streams, lakes, and rivers sooner and with greater energy. That is the root of the stormwater problem.

Of the twenty-six stormwater-impaired streams in the Champlain basin, nineteen flow directly or indirectly into Lake Champlain, including Potash Brook and eleven others in Chittenden County. Stormwater can cause impairment because of the quality of the water delivered to the stream and because of changes in the timing and quantity of discharge. Changes in water quality are probably the easiest to understand. As stormwater moves over impervious surfaces, it picks up everything on those surfaces: motor oil, gasoline, radiator and transmission fluids from leaking cars; dog poop; metals from building materials and cars (brake linings, galvanized steel, tin roofs); litter; pesticides, fertilizers, and grass clippings from lawns; sand and salt from road maintenance; and so on.

Why have no stormwater-impaired streams been identified in the Plattsburgh, New York, area? It may be due to an absence of data, or different standards for classifying stormwater impairment, but there is another, at least partial, explanation. Most of the developed land around Plattsburgh drains directly to the Saranac River, rather than small streams like Potash Brook. Like the Saranac, the Winooski River, which receives some stormwater discharge from Burlington, is not considered stormwater impaired. But why should rivers be different from brooks or streams when it comes to impairment?

Large rivers are less likely to exhibit signs of impairment than small streams. For one thing, it is more difficult to measure the effects of stormwater pollution in large rivers, though they nonetheless occur. Pollution still enters the Winooski and the Saranac from the developed landscape, but the volume of water moving through these rivers can sweep more of the pollutants immediately into Lake Champlain. Impairment may develop subtly, over a longer period. Additionally, impervious surfaces make up much less of the entire drainage area, proportionally, for large rivers than for small streams located entirely in urbanized areas.

Two of the more common pollutants—bacteria and phosphorus—have substantial impacts on Champlain and our ability to enjoy the lake. High bacterial counts have led to beach closures in and around urbanized areas of the Champlain Valley. Bacteria thrive on carbon sources, so certain types of stormwater pollution promote their growth more than others: grass clippings left in the road; litter; and untreated waste from dogs and other animals. While bacteria are limited by a lack of carbon, algae in the water are limited by the availability of phosphorus.

Although explaining the sources of phosphorus in stormwater runoff is a challenge, there is no doubt that it is there. In the Champlain basin, developed land contributes approximately three times more phosphorus per acre than does agricultural land. While we have made substantial gains in managing phosphorus from wastewater treatment plants and agricultural fields, the increased acreage of developed land has largely offset these improvements.

As for where the phosphorus comes from, there are probably many answers, and the sources are not distributed evenly across the developed landscape; but the principal source is erosion. Since the vast majority of phosphorus is held in the top few inches of soil, a little bit of erosion can lead to substantial phosphorus loading. Erosion is augmented in developed areas because of construction activity and changes in stream hydrology due to stormwater runoff.

Again, with unpaved ground, the soil retains water and slowly discharges it to streams over time; the vegetation and uneven surfaces of a natural landscape absorb rainwater's energy, so it is calmed before reaching a stream. Paved surfaces absorb little water, and flow is unimpeded. When fast-flowing stormwater—loaded with sediment and our long list of pollutants from impervious surfaces—reaches a receiving stream, it alters the stream's hydrology in addition to discharging the sediment and pollutants. A larger volume of water flows through the stream in a shorter time. More water with more energy carries more sediment, and phosphorus is bound to the sediment. The stream also picks up sediment from its banks and its bottom. The result is a wider, deeper channel with exposed tree roots along the bank.

Changes in hydrology and increases in sedimentation affect the ability of streams to support aquatic life. Alternating stretches of riffles and pools that provided a diversity of habitats are replaced by wider, deeper, uniform channels. Once the flush of stormwater has passed, the remaining flow cannot fill the new channel; water spreads over a greater area and, in doing so, deposits sediment it was carrying. The sediment fills spaces between cobbles and stones that had offered refuge to crayfish and various insects.

One would think that the effects of stormwater could be mitigated if the water were just held in temporary ponds and then released over time. Indeed, that has been a primary management strategy for stormwater. However, designing and maintaining ponds is challenging. If the pond is too small, a good storm or winter thaw overwhelms its ability to detain water. A pond that is appropriately sized when first built will become less effective if land draining to it is later paved, because more pavement means higher stormwater flows. Without maintenance, ponds fill with sediment and decaying vegetation. Furthermore, pollutants such as metals accumulate in the sediments of the pond. Other stormwater treatment practices have similar limitations.

Stormwater impairment of streams has arisen over the last fifty years as we have transformed our landscape for the benefit of cars. There are now more parking lots and more paved roads. Such development has offered many benefits, including freedom to travel, efficient delivery of goods and services, and more options in where we live. But we are now beginning to recognize the consequences of changing the landscape for the sake of cars. More options in where we live and work often means loss of community, as well as fragmentation of forested parcels and habitat disruption. More traffic means increased air pollution. And, of course, more impervious surface means degradation of water quality. Full recognition of both the benefits and consequences of development patterns may allow us to envision a more sustainable landscape for the future and preserve little havens like Potash Brook.

Land Use: Agriculture

Farmers are often blamed for water pollution problems, but commodity prices, not water quality, drives most farm decisions. A successful farmer must first and foremost run a successful business. Decisions are not made in blatant disregard for water quality or other environmental impacts, but market forces lead farmers to decide what crops to grow, which animals to raise, or how large to get. While callous individuals can be found in any profession, the majority of farmers care greatly about the land and water they tend.

Dairy provides the principal economic force for the Champlain Valley's agriculture. The wet, cold climate of the region works well for growing grass, historically the principal feed source for cows. However, changes in technology and markets in the last few decades have led to a glut of milk on the national market. Massive farms on the West Coast enjoy economies of scale beyond local farmers' dreams.

Low milk prices force difficult decisions. Farmers must produce more to return the same profit. In recent years the Champlain Valley has seen a decrease in the number of dairy farms but little change in the number of cows, meaning the farms that remain have gotten bigger. However, expanding the farm means incurring more debt. If prices continue to fall, interest on debt becomes overwhelming. When ranking factors in deciding whether to expand an operation, most farmers put concerns about water quality low on the list. That is a price society pays for cheap food.

Legislatures and agencies enact laws and policies to ensure that water quality receives at least some consideration in farm-level decisions. Thus, money is allocated to help farmers install fencing to keep animals away from water, or to better manage animal wastes, or to maintain minimal buffer strips between crops and water bodies. Some laws and policies are effective; others suffer from lack of enforcement.

Laws and policies also do not always have the intended effect. For example, to limit the amount of manure going onto the land, an agency could craft a policy regulating how much land was needed for each unit of manure to be spread. An unintended consequence could be the conversion of forestland to agriculture by farmers seeking to find an outlet for the amount of manure their farm is producing.

Ultimately, markets are the swiftest and most powerful force shaping farm practices, and markets have been driving farms to get bigger. On the plus side, bigger farms usually have more resources to invest in environmental conservation practices and better manure management. However, bigger farms tend to rely more heavily on row crops like corn. Compared to pastureland, row crops mean both more erosion and more pesticide use. Also, bigger farms that warehouse cows in large barns lack the charm that comes with black and white Holsteins feeding on a lush green hillside backed by brilliant blue skies.

Small-scale farming can succeed only if countervailing market forces develop. Changing the habits of consumers so that they buy local products is the first, logical step. When farmers can depend on a steady income from local sales, the need to increase farm size to produce more of a single commodity lessens. Local consumers usually seek a diversity of products from a farm, rather than large amounts of a single product.

At present, farm stands and farmers' markets offer the most common sources for local produce. Here consumers can mingle with local growers while scrutinizing their produce. Farmers' markets offer the additional advantage of allowing comparisons between different farms' products. Cooperative markets frequently emphasize local products as well.

Community supported agriculture (CSA) offers another opportunity for purchasing local products and provides an even more reliable source of income for the grower. With CSAs the consumer purchases a share of a farm's annual production. At regular intervals the consumer can then go to the farm and pick up a portion of what has been harvested.

Of course, the short growing season means farmers' markets and CSAs aren't an option year-round. They can also be more expensive. On the other hand, the food is fresher and therefore tastes better, and buying local food is probably the most important step consumers can take toward reducing their own impact on the environment, short of giving up their car. And CSA members can actually see how the farm is managed—it's not a hidden factor. If two farms sell the same product and consumers know one is managed better than the other, they can let their dollars reflect that difference. Instead of paying a hidden ecological cost for cheap food, consumers pay a transparent economic cost for good, healthy food. Eating locally is but one of many ways individuals can have a positive effect on their environment.

Invasive Species

In Shakespeare's *Romeo and Juliet*, Juliet laments the family feud that keeps her from her lover. If only Romeo had a different name, their union would be easier, and Juliet wonders, "What's in a name? That which we call a rose by any other word would smell as sweet." But as she is painfully aware, names do matter. For example, the simple task of categorizing a species as "exotic" or "invasive" influences public perception and how a species is managed.

For a species to be deemed invasive, it must meet two criteria, according to an executive order guiding U.S. government policy. First, it must be "nonnative" or alien to the ecosystem being considered. Second, the species must cause or be likely to cause economic or environmental harm or harm to human health.

Species in Lake Champlain that meet both criteria are well known. Water chestnut and Eurasian water milfoil clog waterways and bays, making navigation and recreation difficult and displacing native plants. Zebra mussels have outcompeted many native mussel species and cause economic harm by coating water intake pipes. Alewives certainly have the potential to be invasive.

Other species not yet here also have the potential to cause economic or environmental harm. Round goby, a fish species, have invaded the Great Lakes. They are a voracious predator of fish eggs and have been implicated in the spread of avian botulism, which on Lakes Erie and Ontario has killed scores of birds, including loons, gulls, and ducks. The botulism toxin accumulates in mussels upon which the gobies feed. Though not immune to the toxin, the gobies can survive for a period of time, during which they are susceptible to predation from birds. Other worrisome potential invaders include the spiny water flea and the fishhook water flea. These two zooplankton species have invaded the Great Lakes, where they replace other plankton species. Their long spiny tails make them unpalatable to fish. So far, Lake Champlain's zooplankton community has not been greatly impacted by competition from invaders, but arrival of either of these water fleas would likely change that.

Species that are nonnative but not necessarily harmful often slip under the radar. Dandelions provide a terrestrial example of a species that has become "naturalized." Although they arrived from Europe with the colonists, they have essentially fit into the ecological landscape, neither displacing native species nor growing with wild abandon (though fastidious lawn managers may disagree).

Some nonnative species are actively cultivated. Crops like wheat and soy are examples. In Lake Champlain, fisheries managers intentionally add enormous numbers of nonnative species. In 2005 the New York and Vermont Departments of Environmental Conservation stocked over 120,000 brown trout (native to Europe) and steelhead (native to the American West) directly into Lake Champlain and many more in tributaries to the lake.

Natural range expansion can bring new native species into the ecosystem of the lake. Double-crested cormorants have undergone substantial natural range expansion. They were unknown on Lake Champlain prior to the early 1980s, but today they abound. However, since they are natives, they cannot be considered invasive.

Sea lamprey, once thought to be exotic, are native to Lake Champlain, thus they do not fit the definition of an invasive species. Yet, sea lamprey are treated as a nuisance, and hundreds of thousands of dollars are expended each year in a campaign to limit their numbers. Sea lamprey are blamed for difficulties in reestablishing populations of lake trout and salmon—native predators whose populations in Lake Champlain were decimated by the early 1900s by overfishing and loss of habitat to dams. At the peak of the sea lamprey population, as many as 90 percent of lake trout and salmon bore scars from sea lamprey wounds. However, the stocked fish in the lake today are of a different genetic strain and perhaps have lost some ability to avoid or combat sea lamprey. Additionally, approximately 40 percent of the salmonids stocked directly into Lake Champlain are nonnative species (brown trout and steelhead), and they create competition for the lake trout and salmon, as well as a food source for the sea lamprey.

Sea lamprey are not the first species to have their origin disputed. The Lake Champlain Basin Program's fish species list defines rainbow smelt as native to the lake, but the U.S. Geological Survey has a Web site that lists them as nonnative. Rainbow smelt have been purposefully introduced to some freshwater systems, but, like sea lamprey, they may have migrated to Lake Champlain after the retreat of the glaciers. In any event, they are currently the dominant forage fish here and thus an integral component of the ecosystem. No one would refer to them as a nuisance.

Eelgrass (*Vallisneria americana*) is another native species sometimes considered a nuisance. For those interested only in boating and swimming, a weed is a weed is a weed, and eelgrass can wrap around propellers and interfere with swimming as easily as Eurasian water milfoil. However, eelgrass plays a valuable ecological role, offering an excellent source of food for ducks and other waterfowl and serving as a haven for myriad invertebrates that provide food for fish. Thus, eelgrass demonstrates the importance of understanding a species before blindly attempting to manage it.

Of those exotic species whose origin of introduction to Lake Champlain is known, over 60 percent entered via canals, particularly the Champlain Canal. Many more species stand poised to join them. The Hudson River has over twice as many exotic species as Lake Champlain; the Great Lakes host almost four times more.

The Champlain Canal first opened in 1823, promising, and providing, extensive commercial connection between the resources of the North Country and the markets and manufacturers of Montreal and New York. Near its heyday in 1890, the canal carried over 1.5 million tons of commercial freight annually. As recently as 1988, over 250,000 tons of commercial goods still passed through each year. Since then, however, commercial traffic has withered. Less than 1 percent of the 1988 tonnage transited the canal in 2004.

Exotic invaders can leak in slowly, over time; there is often an opportunity to halt their progress. A report on potential barriers to nuisance species in the canal considered six methods of dealing with the threat of new nuisance species, including doing nothing. Some of the other options would have limited effectiveness. For example, biological controls in the canal such as added predators or pathogens would be species-specific rather than broadly applicable. Similarly, barriers such as electric currents through the water would not be effective at preventing plants from passing through the canal, though they have been used in other systems for targeted fish species control. In some cases, the ecological costs of a strategy are too steep. Modifying the chemical conditions of the water by adding pesticides or changing the pH would have unacceptable impacts on nontarget species. As for closing the canal completely, economic arguments convinced the authors the strategy was impractical. The best option, the authors suggest, is modifying the canal for a short stretch so that smaller boats would need to be transported but the canal locks could remain operational for limited commercial traffic. This option would allow the most protection from future nuisance species invasions, with the fewest economic and ecological impacts.

Education may provide the best means of closing other portals to introductions. Species can come in as hitchhikers on fishing gear, boats, or trailers. Thorough cleaning of such gear when moving from one water body to another can limit such dispersals.

Global Warming

Factors that influence the future of Lake Champlain extend well beyond what happens locally. Changes in the regional or even global climate will affect the lake as well.

By now the concept of global warming is familiar even to schoolchildren, but acceptance of the reality of large-scale, human-induced climate change has been a long time coming. In 1896 a Swedish physical chemist, Svante Arrhenius, was trying to explain why the earth sometimes got cool enough to cause ice ages. He was the first to suggest that global climate might be altered if there were changes in the amount of carbon dioxide in the layer of gases that insulate the planet. Until the mid-1930s, no one really considered the possibility that temperatures might also increase if carbon dioxide concentrations increased; but around that time anecdotal evidence of wide-scale temperature increases began to accumulate. (Incidentally, the first recorded instance of Lake Champlain not freezing over in two subsequent years was 1932 and 1933.)

Still, most researchers dismissed even the possibility that human activities could influence the climate. Their dismissal was based primarily on two assumptions: first, that oceans would absorb all the excess carbon dioxide, and second, that carbon dioxide couldn't really absorb much heat. However, after World War II, new technologies allowed both these assumptions to be tested, and scientists found them to be false.

"Since the early 1960s, virtually all scientists have accepted that the level of carbon dioxide in the atmosphere is rising, and that the extra gas must intercept some outgoing infrared radiation and so change the distribution of heat in the atmosphere," wrote Spencer Weart in a review of the history of global warming research for *Physics Today* in 1997. Both the U.N.-sponsored Intergovernmental Panel on Climate Change (IPCC) and the National Research Council of the National Academy of Sciences—commissioned by the George W. Bush administration to review the IPCC's findings—have stated that global warming caused by human-induced increases of carbon dioxide is occurring now, and that the rate of warming is likely to accelerate in the years to come.

Despite the consensus on warming, lingering uncertainties have fueled critics and skeptics. How much carbon dioxide will be absorbed by trees and crops? Will increased water vapor from evaporation lead to less warming (since clouds tend to cause cooling) or more warming (since water, like carbon dioxide, insulates the planet)? What portion of the current warming is caused by humans and what portion might be occurring naturally? "The problem for the skeptics, however, is that they still lack a coherent story about how the atmosphere is working. And whenever they can find any uncertainty in the way that the atmosphere works, they tend to use this to claim that there will be no problem with greenhouse warming," wrote Fred Pearce in a review of the scientific debates around global warming for *New Scientist* magazine. Resolution of uncertainty and assumptions in current models is equally likely to suggest even greater warming might occur.

Responding to massive ecological changes like global warming requires, first, actions to avert or lessen the change, and then adaptation to new conditions if the actions are ineffective. Knowledge of potential future conditions helps us prepare for adaptation. So what might be the ecological consequences of global warming for Lake Champlain?

Warming can bring about physical, chemical, and biological changes in the lake. While some of the physical and chemical changes are fairly straightforward, others are speculative. Potential biological changes are more difficult to predict.

Physical changes mostly involve the temperature of the lake. Higher winter temperatures mean reductions in winter ice cover. Such reductions have already begun. Between 1816 (the first year for which records are available) and 1950, there was a 4 percent to 5 percent chance that the lake would not freeze in a given year. Since 1950 the probability of an unfrozen lake has increased tenfold. Higher temperatures mean the lake will stratify earlier in

Global warming may affect recreational opportunities. (photo by Carolyn L. Bates)

the spring, setting up a warm layer of water over a colder, deeper layer, and stay stratified longer. A 1979 study stated stratification in the Main Lake typically began in early June. Between 2004 and 2007, however, stratification began in early to mid-May.

Higher temperatures and a lack of ice cover mean increased evaporation from the lake. There is a general agreement, at least in models of the Great Lakes, that such increased evaporation means average water levels will fall. However, changes in local precipitation patterns greatly influence water levels, and such changes may differ between the Great Lakes region and the Champlain Valley.

Most computer models predict an increase in precipitation in the Northeast if global temperatures rise. Furthermore, the intensity of precipitation events is likely to increase, meaning more rains of one inch or more. More intense storms will mean increases in flooding and erosion-related runoff. More erosion will mean more nutrient delivery to the lake. A 2006 report from the state of Vermont notes, "the especially high [phosphorus] loading rates during certain intervals . . . can be primarily attributed to wetter weather patterns producing high runoff rates during those years."

Chemically, decreases in the oxygen content of lake water are likely, since warm water holds less oxygen than cold water. Additionally, the longer duration of summer stratification would increase the likelihood of oxygen depletion in lower layers. Such oxygen depletion now occurs fairly regularly in the Inland Sea.

Predicting biological changes in the lake as a result of warming means attempting to integrate the impacts of all the physical and chemical changes on each species and speculating about how they will affect each species' interactions with other species.

Observed effects to date in other lakes have sometimes been contradictory. In Arctic lakes, global warming has led to an increase in algal biomass due to longer growing seasons. On the other hand, in Lake Tanganyika in Africa algal production has decreased because warmer weather and less wind have meant less nutrient delivery to the water.

Some interactions are more complicated. In Lake Washington near Seattle, algae and their predators used to reach population maximums at about the same time each year. Now, however, higher temperatures allow the algae to bloom earlier in the summer, but the predators have not adapted. The predator population has fallen by more than half since the late 1970s.

Fish, too, will need to adapt to changing temperatures. Spawning in many species is triggered by optimum temperatures. Earlier warming would mean earlier spawning. Perhaps more important, available habitat for cold-water species like trout and salmon could decrease, while habitat for warm-water species like bass could increase.

While global warming has begun, and preliminary effects have been observed in Lake Champlain, scientists mostly agree there is still a small window of opportunity for minimizing future warming. For decades Americans have shunned steps that would help avoid future warming: driving less, developing alternative fuel sources, increasing vehicle fuel efficiency, investing in energy efficiency. Without speedy adoption of strategies like these, we will be left only the option of adaptation.

○ The Value of the Lake

As the sun dips toward the Adirondack Mountains, a small girl stands at the water's edge wearing a baseball cap and pink sweatshirt and holding a fishing pole. Suddenly the pole arcs with the weight of a sunfish struggling at the end of the line, her first ever. What is the value of the smile that bursts across her face?

Early morning dawns as the cattails brim with life. A slight mist rises from the placid lake. A kayak blade dips quietly into the water as the boat skims the surface. What is the value of the marsh wrens' rattling songs, or the booming *galump-a-lump* of an American bittern resounding through the still air? Are they worth less if the kayaker isn't there?

A full moon hangs in the sky, giving rise to a trail of light dancing across the water. On shore, a campfire crackles while the hearty laughter of good friends rolls across the lake. How much are camaraderie and joy worth?

Cervantes wrote, "That which costs little is less valued," and sometimes I fear our perception of the lake verifies his words. Is it only when we as a society begin pouring resources into cleaning the lake, to counteract decades of abuse, that we come to value the treasures it offers apart from any economic return? Is it only after we associate a cost with clean water that we really come to appreciate its benefits?

Economists can generate models and estimates of the value of an ecological system. They ask questions like, how much money is spent by tourists? how much is a clean drinking-water source for over 200,000 people worth? how much more valuable is property on the water compared to similar property far from the water? how much value does the lake add to chocolatiers, baseball teams, or chambers of commerce that trade on its image? More intrinsic values face withering scrutiny before the cold-eyed realism of economics. To even be considered they must be cloaked in terms like "contingent values," "option values," or "existence values"—terms that help put a dollar sign on in-place ecosystems.

More recently, economists at the University of Vermont have tried to work ecosystem services into their models. So, for example, they estimate how much value a large lake's ability to moderate temperatures provides to society, or how much it would cost to filter water in the absence of the wetlands around the lake that now do the job for free. Such models are a vast improvement over those that simply discount ecosystem services as intrinsic and valueless. Still, there is an old saying among modelers: "All models are wrong; some models are useful."

I'm not sure how useful any of the models of the economic value of Lake Champlain might be, but I know their estimates are wrong. They must consistently underestimate the lake's value. Models can't begin to account for the true worth of a resource that can generate a young girl's smile, a bird's song, or laughter among friends. Anyone who has spent any time on the lake can surely come up with a host of intangible, valuable, but undervalued assets.

The intangible values Lake Champlain offers differ from most economic benefits in exquisite ways. Intangibles are renewable. Smiles can be generated over and over without risk of depleting the resource; so too with laughter. Intangibles can be accumulated irrespective of income. Though wealth may improve an individual's access, the lake is a common resource available to all. A poor man and a rich man can simultaneously partake of a refreshing swim in the lake.

The intangible values endear the lake to those who play and live in and around it. At the end of the day, you remember the swimming, not the cost of parking at the beach. You remember the fish caught and the sites seen, not the price of the fishing license and bait. You remember the waves lapping against the side of the boat and a gentle breeze, not the cost of the outing. Economists' figures capture but a shadow of the truth. Memories and experiences supply the better part of the lake's true value.

THE INDIVIDUAL'S ROLE

My little sister has always been self-conscious about her weight. I think it is partly my fault. When we were growing up she would regularly ask, "Does this outfit make me look fat?" Without even looking I would answer "yes," in the hope that she would stop bothering me. I cannot do that anymore. She has lost over thirty pounds. She made a pledge to herself and in front of others that she would take off the weight, and she stuck to it. She had to eat less and exercise more, but the effort paid off, and she looks and feels great.

Lake Champlain could stand to eat less, too; right now the lake takes in excess food (in the form of phosphorus) each year. Instead of the food showing up as fat, it gets expressed as algae blooms. Just as extra weight in a person is not necessarily distributed evenly, the excess nutrients in Lake Champlain are concentrated more in some parts of the lake than others. Lake Champlain really shows its extra weight in the shallow northern bays.

Unfortunately, the lake cannot diet by itself. The lake does not really have much control over what it eats; that is the responsibility of those of us who live within its watershed. We need to stop feeding it so much.

Some of the nutrients and other pollutants come from our own homes and driveways. Every time excess soil erodes from a lawn, every time water zips across a driveway rather than percolating into the soil, every time too much fertilizer is spread on the grass, every time our pets poop outside on the sidewalk, more nutrients can get into the lake.

There are many simple actions that can be taken to minimize excess pollution. To prevent erosion around the house, reseed bare patches of ground or make sure gutter spouts discharge to vegetated areas rather than pavement. Avoid using fertilizer unless a soil test (from a cooperative extension or a garden supply store) indicates your lawn actually needs it. Better yet, eliminate some or all of your lawn and replace it with a wildflower meadow or some ground-cover plants that would eliminate the need for fertilizers. Pick up your pet's poop and flush it down the toilet. Landscape in ways that allow water to percolate into the soil rather than running immediately off the property.

The Lake Champlain Committee (LCC) has compiled a list of such actions that anyone can take to help put the lake on a diet, and limit household toxics. LCC has spent innumerable hours helping state and local agencies craft effective policies to better protect our lake. Yet, no policies in the world can be effective on their own if individual citizens do not take responsibility for their personal actions. Still, any dieter knows even small behavior changes can be difficult to maintain. The secret to successful dieting is sharing your goals with others. That is why we ask people to make a public commitment, a pledge, to help protect Lake Champlain. This is not a pledge of money. It is simply a public commitment to adopt practices around your home that are most protective of water quality.

To take the pledge visit www.lakechamplaincommittee.org. There you can find a list of actions individuals can take and a form to fill out signifying that you are willing to do your part. Sign up and then pass the word on to friends and family. If enough people pledge to change the things within their own control, we can shed excess tons from the lake's diet.

Sunset, Burlington Pier (photo by Carolyn L. Bates)

RESOURCES / BIBLIOGRAPHY

Sources consulted are listed by chapter and section, in alphabetical order by author, editor, or organization serving as author.

1. THE SETTING

The Origin of Lake Champlain

Ansley, Jane E. *Topography of the Northeastern US: A Brief Review*. Paleontological Research Institute, 2000. http://www.priweb.org/ed/TFGuide/NE/topo/topo_files2/topo_pdfs/ne_topo2.pdf (accessed November 2007).

Doolan, Barry. "The Geology of Vermont." *Rocks and Minerals* 71 (1996): 218–25.

Johnson, Charles W. *The Nature of Vermont: Introduction and Guide to a New England Environment.* Hanover, NH: University Press of New England, 1998.

Myer, G. E., and G. K. Gruendling. *Limnology of Lake Champlain.* Burlington, VT: Lake Champlain Basin Study, New England River Basins Commission, 1979.

Pielou, E. C. *After the Ice Age: The Return of Life to Glaciated North America.* Chicago: University of Chicago Press, 1991.

Wright, S. F. "Glacial Geology of the Burlington Colchester 7.5' Quadrangle, Northern Vermont," 2003. http://www.anr.state.vt.us/dec/geo/pdfdocs/GlacGeoBurlwright.pdf (accessed August 2007).

The Sixth Great Lake

Great Lakes Commission policy position, 1998: designation of Lake Champlain as a Great Lake. http://www.glc.org/announce/98/03champ.html (accessed November 2007).

Grondahl, Paul. "Sizing up Lake Champlain." *Albany Times Union*, March 8, 1998.

In Lakes, Does Size Matter?

Hutchinson, George Evelyn. *Treatise on Limnology*, vol. 1, *Geography, Physics, and Chemistry*. London: John Wiley & Sons, 1957.

International Lake Environment Committee. "Lake Champlain," 1999. http://www.ilec.or.jp/database/nam/nam-38.html (accessed November 2007).

Myer and Gruendling, *Limnology of Lake Champlain.*

Downhill Looking Up

Champlain quote translation from http://www.pc.gc.ca/lhn-nhs/qc/fortchambly/natcul/natcul2a_e.asp. A translation of the *Voyages of Samuel de Champlain* (E. F. Slater, ed., Boston: Prince Society, 1878) can be found online at http://historiclakes.org/S_de_Champ/Champlain25.html.

Myer and Gruendling, *Limnology of Lake Champlain.*

Five Lakes in One

Myer and Gruendling, *Limnology of Lake Champlain.*

Shanley, J. B., and J. C. Denner. "The Hydrology of the Lake Champlain Basin." From *Lake Champlain in Transition from Research toward Restoration*, Thomas O. Manley and Patricia L. Manley, eds. Washington, DC: American Geophysical Union, 1999.

A Tale of Two Bays

"Jewel of New England" quote from press release from office of U.S. Sen. Patrick Leahy, 2004. Sens. Leahy and Jeffords introduce bill to set the stage for Lake Champlain's 400th anniversary. http://leahy.senate.gov/press/200407/072304.html (accessed November 2007).

"Ecological disaster" quote from "Listen to the Dire Warning of Missisquoi Bay." *Burlington Free Press.* December 15, 2003. http://www.burlingtonfreepress.com/specialnews/lake/16.htm (accessed November 2007).

Myer and Gruendling, *Limnology of Lake Champlain.*

2. FORCES

Retention Time

Shanley and Denner, "The Hydrology of the Lake Champlain Basin."

Catching a Wave

Jessey, David R. "Oceanography II: Waves," 1998. http://geology.csupomona.edu/drjessey/class/Gsc101/OceanographyII.html (accessed November 2007).

Knowles, Ernest. "Changes in Wave Direction," 2003. http://www4.ncsu.edu/eos/users/c/ceknowle/public/chapter10/part4.html (accessed November 2007).

Autumn's Mix-up

Garrison, Ronnie. "Fall Turnover," 1997. http://fishing.about.com/library/weekly/aa091597.htm (accessed November 2007).

International Lake Environment Committee, "Lake Champlain."

Myer and Gruendling, *Limnology of Lake Champlain*.

Water on the Web, 2006. http://waterontheweb.org/under/lakeecology/index.html (accessed November 2007).

Slosh, Slosh

Manley, T. O., K. L. Hunkins, J. H. Saylor, G. S. Miller, and P. L. Manley. "Aspects of Summertime and Wintertime Hydrodynamics of Lake Champlain." In *Lake Champlain in Transition from Research toward Restoration*, Thomas O. Manley and Patricia L. Manley, eds. Washington, DC: American Geophysical Union, 1999.

Wuest, A., and D. M. Farmer. "Seiche." In *Encyclopaedia of Science and Technology*, 9th ed. McGraw-Hill, 2001. http://www.eawag.ch/research_e/apec/Scripts/Seiche-612800.pdf (accessed November 2007).

Let There Be Light

Hutchinson, *Treatise on Limnology*, vol. 1.

Hutchinson, George Evelyn. *A Treatise on Limnology*, vol. 2, *Introduction to Lake Biology and Limnoplankton*. London: John Wiley & Sons, 1967.

Water on the Web, 2006.

Lake Ice

Barnes, Peter W. "Marine and Lacustrine Sedimentary Processes Involving Non-Glacial Ice." *Proceedings of the U.S. Geological Survey Sediment Workshop February 4–7, 1997*. http://water.usgs.gov/osw/techniques/workshop/barnes.html (accessed November 2007).

Claussen, Van. "Ice Safety," 2005. http://www.inquiry.net/outdoor/winter/health/ice_safety.htm (accessed November 2007).

Libbrecht, Kenneth G. "Snow Crystals," 1999. http://www.its.caltech.edu/~atomic/snowcrystals/ (accessed November 2007).

Spadaccini, Jim. "Skating," 1997. http://www.exploratorium.com/hockey/skating1.html (accessed November 2007).

U.S. Department of Agriculture. Stream Systems Technology Center, 1996. http://www.stream.fs.fed.us/news/streamnt/jul96/jul96a6.htm (accessed November 2007).

Understanding Your River

Mississippi State University Agricultural & Biological Engineering. *Stream Corridor Restoration: Principles, Practices, and Processes*, 1998. http://www.abe.msstate.edu/csd/strm-cor-res/index.php (accessed November 2007).

Vermont Department of Environmental Conservation. "Vermont Stream Geomorphic Assessment Protocols," 2007. http://www.vtwaterquality.org/rivers/htm/rv_geoassesspro.htm (accessed November 2007).

3. PHENOMENA

Thick Frothy Foam

Courtemanch, David. "Foam—A Cause for Concern?" *Maine Fish and Game Magazine*, 1979. http://www.maine.gov/dep/blwq/doclake/foam.htm (accessed November 2007).

Fuller, Doug. "The Occurrence of Foam on Lakes and Streams," 2003. http://www.greatlakesdirectory.org/zarticles/012903_great_lakes1.htm (accessed November 2007).

Streaking

Malinen, T., J. Horppila, and A. Liljendahl-Nurminen. "Langmuir Circulations Disturb the Low-Oxygen Refuge of Phantom Midge Larvae." *Limnological Oceanography* 46(3) (2001): 689–92.

Phillips, W. R. C. "Langmuir Circulations." In *Wind over Waves II: Forecasting and Fundamentals of Applications*, S. G. Sajjadi and Julian C. R. Hunt, eds. Oxford University Press, 2002.

In a Fog

Federal Emergency Management Association and National Oceanic and Atmospheric Association. *Hazardous Weather Resource Guide*, 1996. http://www.ih2000.net/jasperem/NOAA%20Hazardous%20Weather%20Guide.pdf (accessed November 2007).

Mirages

Heirdorn, Keith C. "The Superior Mirage: Seeing Beyond," 1999. http://www.islandnet.com/~see/weather/elements/supmrge.htm (accessed November 2007).

Hutchinson, *Treatise on Limnology*, vol. 1.

Let It Snow

Tardy, Alexander. "Lake Effect and Lake Enhanced Snow in the Champlain Valley of Vermont," 2000. Eastern Region Technical Attachment No. 2000-05.

The General

Manley, P. L., T. O. Manley, M. C. Watzin, and J. Gutierrez. "Lakebed Pockmarks in Burlington Bay, Lake Champlain—I. Hydrodynamics and Implications of Origin." In *Lake Champlain: Partnerships and Research in the New Millennium*, Tom O. Manley, Pat L. Manley, and Timothy B. Mihuc, eds. New York: Kluwer Academic / Plenum Publishers, 2004.

Watzin, M. C., P. L. Manley, T. O. Manley, and S. A. Kyriakeas. "Lakebed Pockmarks in Burlington Bay, Lake Champlain—II. Habitat Characteristics and Biological Patterns." In *Lake Champlain: Partnerships and Research in the New Millennium*, Tom O. Manley, Pat L. Manley, and Timothy B. Mihuc, eds. New York: Kluwer Academic / Plenum Publishers, 2004.

4. LIVING LAKE: PLANTS

Where Land Meets Water

Delta

Axelsson, Valter. "Formation of River Deltas." http://home.swipnet.se/valter/df.html (accessed November 2007).

Lake Champlain Basin Program. *Lake Champlain Basin Atlas: Version 3.0.* (2004). http://www.lcbp.org/Atlas/index.htm (accessed November 2007).

Beach

National Oceanic and Atmospheric Association. *Beach Nourishment: A Guide for Local Government Officials,* 2007. http://www.csc.noaa.gov/beachnourishment/index.htm (accessed November 2007).

Cedar Bluffs

Peattie, Donald Culross. *A Natural History of Trees of Eastern and Central North America.* Boston: Houghton Mifflin, 1991.

Thompson, Elizabeth H., and Eric R. Sorenson. *Wetland, Woodland, Wildland: A Guide to the Natural Communities of Vermont.* Vermont Fish & Wildlife Department and The Nature Conservancy; Hanover, NH: University Press of New England (distributor), 2000.

Falling Leaves: Investing in the Food Chain

Vannote, R. L., G. W. Minshall, K. W. Cummins, J. R. Sedell, and C. E. Cushing. "The River Continuum Concept." *Canadian Journal of Fisheries and Aquatic Sciences* 37(1) (1980): 130–37.

Putting Away the Groceries: Food Storage in Lake Champlain

Big Muskego Lake / Bass Bay Protection and Rehabilitation District Commissioners. "Big Muskego Lake and Bass Bay Management Plan." City of Muskego, WI, 2004.

Meijer, Marie-Louise. "Biomanipulation in the Netherlands: 15 Years of Experience." PhD diss. Wageningen (Netherlands) University, 2000.

Scheffer, Marten. "Searching Explanations of Nature in the Mirror World of Math." *Conservation Ecology* 3(2) (1999): 11. http://www.consecol.org/vol3/iss2/art11 (accessed November 2007).

Water Plants

Reimer, Donald N. *Introduction to Freshwater Vegetation.* Westport, CT: AVI Publishing, 1984.

Blue-green Algae: What's the Risk?

Boyer, G. L., M. C. Watzin, A. D. Shambaugh, M. F. Satchwell, B. H. Rosen, and T. Mihuc. "The Occurrence of Cyanobacteria Toxins in Lake Champlain." In *Lake Champlain: Partnerships and Research in the New Millennium*, Tom O. Manley, Pat L. Manley, and Timothy B. Mihuc, eds. New York: Kluwer Academic / Plenum Publishing, 2004.

Chorus, Ingrid, and Jamie Bartram, eds. *Toxic Cyanobacteria in Water: A Guide to Their Public Health Consequences, Monitoring and Management.* London: World Health Organization, 1999.

Little Glass Houses

Charles, D. F. "Relationship between Surface Sediment Diatom Assemblages and Lake Water Characteristics in Adirondack Lakes." *Ecology* 66(3) (1985): 994–1011.

Hutchinson, *Treatise on Limnology*, vol. 2.

5. LIVING LAKE: ANIMALS

A Night for the Birds

Bull, John L. *Birds of New York State* (including the 1976 supplemental). Ithaca, NY: Cornell University Press, 1986.

Duerr, Adam E. "Population Dynamics, Foraging Ecology, and Optimal Management of Double-Crested Cormorants on Lake Champlain." PhD diss. University of Vermont, 2007.

Laughlin, Sarah B., and Douglas P. Kibbe, eds. *The Atlas of Breeding Birds of Vermont*. Hanover, NH: University Press of New England, 1985.

Dumpster Divers and Glorious Birds

Audubon, John James. *Birds of America*, vol 7. New York and Philadelphia: J. J. Audubon, 1840.

Bent, Arthur Cleveland. *Life Histories of North American Gulls and Terns*. New York: Dover, 1921.

Blokpoel, H., and G. D. Tessier. *The Ring-Billed Gull in Ontario: A Review of a New Problem Species*. Ottawa: Canadian Wildlife Service, 1986.

Samuels, Edward A. *Ornithology and Oology of New England: Containing Full Descriptions of the Birds of New England, and Adjoining States and Provinces*. Boston: Nichols and Noyes, 1867.

Spear, Robert N. Jr. "Wildlife: Part II. Birds." *Lake Champlain Basin Studies*. Frederic O. Sargent, Alphonse H. Gilbert, and M. Yvonne Gratton, eds. A compilation of studies sponsored by America the Beautiful Fund, Chittenden County (VT) Regional Planning Commission, University of Vermont Department of Resource Economics and the university's Extension Service, and the Lake Champlain Committee: Burlington, VT, 1972.

Just Passing Through

Batt, Bruce, ed. "The Greater Snow Goose: Report of the Arctic Goose Habitat Working Group." *Arctic Goose Joint Venture Special Publication*. Washington, DC, and Ottawa: U.S. Fish and Wildlife Service and Canadian Wildlife Service, 1998.

Boyd, H., ed. "Population Modeling and Management of Snow Geese," occasional paper no. 102. Canadian Wildlife Service, 1999.

Heyland, J. D., A. Reed, and E. T. Reed. "Greater Snow Goose." Canadian Wildlife Service and Canadian Wildlife Federation, 2003. http://www.hww.ca/hww2.asp?id=44 (accessed November 2007).

Links in the Chain

Post, David M., Michael L. Pace, and Nelson G. Hairston Jr. "Ecosystem Size Determines Food-Chain Length in Lakes." *Nature* 405 (2000): 1047–49.

Something Fishy

Langdon, Rich W., Mark T. Ferguson, and Ken M. Cox. *Fishes of Vermont*. Waterbury: Vermont Fish & Wildlife Department, 2006.

Stephen, D., et al. "Continental-Scale Patterns of Nutrient and Fish Effects on Shallow Lakes: Introduction to a Pan-European Mesocosm Experiment. *Freshwater Biology* 49(12) (2004): 1517–24.

Fish Flu

Durborow, Robert M., Ronald L. Thune, John P. Hawke, and A. C. Camus. "Columnaris Disease: A Bacterial Infection Caused by *Flavobacterium columnare*." Southern Regional Aquaculture Center Publication No. 479 (1998).

Hulburt, Phillip J. "Whirling Disease: A Resource Stewardship Challenge." *Fisheries* 21(6) (1996). http://www.dec.ny.gov/animals/21665.html (accessed January 2008).

Jones, Tom. "Disease Documented in Lake Champlain Northern Pike." Vermont Agency of Natural Resources press release, 2002.

Jones, Tom. "Esocid Lymphosarcoma." Vermont fish health fact sheet. Vermont Agency of Natural Resoues, 2004. http://www.vtfishandwildlife.com/library/Factsheets/Fisheries/Fish_health/Esocid_Lymphosarcoma.pdf (accessed January 2008).

New York State Department of Environmental Conservation. "Viral Hemorrhagic Septicemia (VHS) in New York," 2008. http://www.dec.ny.gov/animals/25328.html (accessed January 2008).

Salmonid Challenges

The Known: Sea Lamprey

Bryan, M. B., D. Zalinski, K. B. Filcek, S. Libants, W. Li, and K. T. Scribner. Patterns of Invasion and Colonization of the Sea Lamprey (*Petromyzon marinus*) in North America as Revealed by Microsatellite Genotypes." *Molecular Ecology* 14 (2005): 3757–73.

Docker, M. F., N. E. Mandrak, D. D. Heath, and K. T. Scribner. "Genetic Markers to Distinguish and Quantify the Level of Gene

Flow between Northern Brook and Silver Lampreys." Ann Arbor, MI: Great Lakes Fishery Commission, Project Completion Report, 2005.

New York State Department of Environmental Conservation and U.S. Fish and Wildlife Service. "Use of Lampricides in a Temporary Program of Sea Lamprey Control in Lake Champlain with an Assessment of Effects on Certain Fish Populations and Sportsfisheries." Final Environmental Impact Statement, 1990.

U.S. Fish and Wildlife Service. "A Long-term Program of Sea Lamprey Control in Lake Champlain." Final Supplemental Environmental Impact Statement, 2001. http://www.fws.gov/r5lcfwro/lampreyeis.pdf (accessed November 2007).

The New: Alewives

Harman, Willard N. "Trophic Changes Following the Introduction of the Alewife in Otsego Lake, NY." In *Lake Champlain Alewife Impacts February 14, 2006 Workshop Summary*, 2006. http://www.uvm.edu/~seagrant/communications/assets/AlewifeSummary.pdf (accessed November 2007).

Mills, E. L., R. O'Gorman, J. DeGisi, R. F. Heberger, and R. A. House. "Food of the Alewife (*Alosa pseudoharengus*) in Lake Ontario before and after the Establishment of *Blythotrephes cederstroemi*." *Canadian Journal of Fisheries and Aquatic Science* 49 (1992): 2009–19.

The Mystery: Where Are the Young?

Ellrott, B. J., and J. E. Marsden. "Lake Trout Reproduction in Lake Champlain." *Transactions of the American Fisheries Society* 133 (2004): 252–64.

Holding an Eel by the Tail

Denoncourt, Charles E., and Jay R. Stauffer Jr. "Feeding Selectivity of the American Eel *Anguilla rostrata* (LeSueur) in the Upper Delaware River." *American Midland Naturalist*, 129(2) (1993): 301–8.

Facey, D. E., and M. J. Van Den Avyle. "Species Profiles: Life Histories and Environmental Requirements of Coastal Fishes and Invertebrates (North Atlantic)—American Eel." *U.S. Fish and Wildlife Service Biological Report* 82(11.74). U.S. Army Corps of Engineers, TR EL-82-4 (1987).

LaBar, G. W., and D. E. Facey. "Local Movements of American Eels (*Anguilla rostrata* LeSueur) in Lake Champlain, Vermont, with Notes on Estimated Population Size." *Transactions of the American Fisheries Society* 112 (1983):111–16.

LaBar, G. W., and D. E. Facey. "Lake Champlain Eels: Ecology and Economics." In *Proceedings of the Seventh Annual Lake Champlain Basin Conference* (1980): 126–37.

Perlmutter, Alfred. "An Aquarium Experiment on the American Eel as a Predator on Larval Lampreys." *Copeia* 1951(2): 173–74. As cited in Potter, I. C. "Ecology of Larval and Metamorphosing Lamprey." *Canadian Journal of Fisheries and Aquatic Science* 37 (1980): 1641–57.

Mishe-Nahma, King of Fishes

Carey, Richard Adams. *The Philosopher Fish: Sturgeon Caviar and the Geography of Desire.* Washington, DC: Counterpoint Press, 2005.

Longfellow, Henry Wadsworth. *The Song of Hiawatha.* London: David Bogue, 1855.

Thompson, Zadock. *History of Vermont, Natural, Civil, and Statistical.* Burlington, VT: Chauncey Goodrich, 1842.

Werner, Robert G. "Contributing Factors in Habitat Selection by Lake Sturgeon (*Acipenser fulvescens*)." Final report submitted to U.S. EPA–Great Lakes National Program Office by the Research Foundation of State University of New York, 2006. http://www.epa.gov/glnpo/ecopage/glbd/LkSturgeon.pdf (accessed November 2007).

Degrees of Separation

Darwin, Charles. *The Origin of Species* (1859). http://www.literature.org/authors/darwin-charles/the-origin-of-species/

Helfield, J. M., and R. J. Naiman. "Effects of Salmon-Derived Nitrogen on Riparian Forest Growth and Implications for Stream Productivity." *Ecology* 82 (2001): 2403–9.

Knight, T. M., M. W. McCoy, J. M. Chase, K. A. McCoy, and R. D. Holt. "Trophic Cascades across Ecosystems." *Nature* 437 (2005): 880–83.

Milgram, Stanley. "Small-World Problem." *Psychology Today* 1 (1) (1967): 61–67.

Ricciardi, Anthony. "Facilitative Interactions among Aquatic Invaders: Is an 'Invasional Meltdown' Occurring in the Great Lakes?" *Canadian Journal of Fisheries and Aquatic Sciences* 58 (2001): 2513–25.

Vanderploeg, H. A., T. F. Nalepa, D. J. Jude, E. L. Mills, K. T. Holeck, J. R. Liebig, I. A. Grigorovich, and H. Ojaveer. "Dispersal and Emerging Ecological Impacts of Ponto-Caspian Species in the Laurentian Great Lakes." *Canadian Journal of Fisheries and Aquatic Sciences* 59(7) (2002): 1209–28.

Mini-Monsters, Little Wheels, Oar Feet, and Prongs

Carling, K. J., T. B. Mihuc, C. Siegfried, R. Bonham, and F. Dunlap. "Where Have All the Rotifers Gone? Zooplankton Community Patterns in Lake Champlain 1992–2001." In *Lake Champlain: Partnerships and Research in the New Millennium*, Tom O. Manley, Pat L. Manley, and Timothy B. Mihuc, eds. New York: Kluwer Academic / Plenum Publishing, 2004.

McIntosh Alan, ed. "Lake Champlain Sediment Toxics Assessment Program." Technical Report #5, Lake Champlain Basin Program: Grand Isle, VT, 1994.

Pennak, Robert W. *Fresh-water Invertebrates of the United States*, 3rd ed. New York: John Wiley & Sons, 1989.

Pothoven, Steve. "Ecology of *Mysis relicta* in the Great Lakes," 2001. http://www.glerl.noaa.gov/res/Task_rpts/2001/edypothoven09-2.html (accessed November 2007).

Stanford, J. A., B. K. Ellis, J. Craft, G. Poole, D. Wicklum, F. Offenkrantz, and C. Stafford. "Food-Web Ecology of Glacial Lakes Invaded by Non-native Mysids and Lake Trout," 2006. http://www.umt.edu/flbs/waterquality/foodwebecology.htm (accessed November 2007).

Home for the Holidays

Bilton, D. T., J. R. Freeland, and B. Okamura. "Dispersal in Freshwater Invertebrates." *Annual Review of Ecology and Systematics* 32 (2001): 159–81.

Cohen, G. M., and J. B. Shurin. "Scale-Dependence and Mechanisms of Dispersal in Freshwater Zooplankton." *Oikos* 103(3) (2003): 603–17.

Figuerola, J., A. J. Green, and T. C. Michot. "Invertebrate Eggs Can Fly: Evidence of Waterfowl-Mediated Gene Flow in Aquatic Invertebrates." *American Naturalist* 165 (2005): 274–80.

Shurin, J. B., and J. E. Havel. "Hydrologic Connections and Overland Dispersal in an Exotic Freshwater Crustacean." *Biological Invasions* 4 (2002): 431–39.

Striding over the Water

Suter, Robert B. "Walking on Water." *American Scientist* 87 (1999): 154–59.

Is a Mussel a Mussel?

U.S. Geological Survey. "Mussels That Matter." Reston, VA: USGS, 1998.

Winhold, Lisa. "Unionidae, Animal Diversity Web," 2004. http://animaldiversity.ummz.umich.edu/site/accounts/information/Unionidae.html (accessed November 2007).

A Long Winter's Nap

Storey, K. B., and J. M. Storey. "Hibernation: Poikilotherms." *Encyclopedia of Life Sciences*. Macmillan Reference Ltd., 2001. www.els.net.

6. THE FUTURE OF LAKE CHAMPLAIN

Periodic Events and Predictability

Harding, J. S., E. F. Benfield, P. V. Bolstad, G. S. Helfman, and E. B. D. Jones III. "Stream Biodiversity: The Ghost of Land-Use Past." *Proceedings of the National Academy of Sciences* 95 (1998): 14843–47.

Noren, A. J., P. B. Bierman, E. J. Steig, A. Lini, and J. Southon. "Millennial-Scale Storminess Variability in the Northeastern United States during Holocene Epoch." *Nature* 419 (2002): 821–24.

Pinsker, Lisa M. "In Search of the Mercury Solution." *Geotimes: Earth, Energy and Environment News* 48(8) (2003): 16–21. http://www.geotimes.org/aug03/feature_mercury.html (accessed November 2007).

Scheffner and Butler. "EST—A New Approach to Frequency Analysis," 1996. As cited in Mandia, Scott A. "Long Island Hurricane Climatology," 2007. http://www2.sunysuffolk.edu/mandias/38hurricane/hurricane_climatology.html (accessed December 2007).

Large-Scale Changes

Land Use: Urban, Suburban

Burton, G. Allen, and Robert Pitt. *Stormwater Effects Handbook: A Toolbox for Watershed Managers, Scientists, and Engineers*. London, New York, Washington, DC, and Boca Raton, LA: Lewis Publishers, 2002.

Fulton, W., R. Pendall, M. Nguyen, and A. Harrison. "Who Sprawls Most? How Growth Patterns Differ across the U.S." Washington, DC: Brookings Institution Center on Urban and Metropolitan Policy, 2001.

RESOURCES/BIBLIOGRAPHY

Invasive Species

Bryan et al., 2005. (see chapter 5, Fish Flu)

Clinton, William J. Executive Order 13112. *Federal Register* 64(25) (1999): 6183–86.

Malchoff, Mark, J. Ellen Marsden, and Michael Hauser. *Feasibility of Champlain Canal Aquatic Nuisance Species Barrier Options.* Sea Grant Lake Champlain, LCSG-01-05 (2005). http://www.uvm.edu/~seagrant/communications/assets/ansbarrierrprt06.pdf (accessed November 2007).

Global Warming

Intergovernmental Panel on Climate Change. *Climate Change 2007: The Physical Science Basis.* Geneva, Switzerland: IPCC Secretariat, 2007.

Pearce, Fred. "Greenhouse Wars." *New Scientist* 2091 (1997): 38. http://www.newscientist.com/article/mg15520915.100-greenhouse-wars.html (accessed November 2007).

Weart, S. "The Discovery of the Risk of Global Warming." *Physics Today* 50(1) (1997): 34–40.

Stocking data from Vermont Fish & Wildlife Department, http://www.vtfishandwildlife.com/fish_stocking.cfm (accessed December 2005), and New York State Department of Environmental Conservation, http://www.dec.state.ny.us/website/dfwmr/fish/stockclin.html (accessed December 2005).

Rainbow smelt information from U.S. Geological Survey, http://nas.er.usgs.gov/queries/FactSheet.asp?speciesID=796 (accessed December 2005), and Lake Champlain Basin Program, www.lcbp.org/factsht/FishSpeciesList.pdf (accessed December 2005).

THE INDIVIDUAL'S ROLE

Lake Champlain Committee. "Help the Lake Take the Pledge," 2003. http://lakechamplaincommittee.org/ (accessed November 2007).

State of Vermont. "The Clean and Clear Action Plan 2006 Annual Report," 2007. http://www.anr.state.vt.us/cleanandclear/rep2006/CleanAndClear2006Rpt.pdf (accessed November 2007).

INDEX

A
agriculture, 21, 70, 127, 129–31
air temperatures, 25, 48, 49, 51–53, 135–36
alewives, 90–91, 98–101, 131
algae
　environmental factors, 18–21, 69–70, 136, 139
　food chain, 68–70, 92–93, 100, 107
　species, 34–35, 73–77, 92, 122
　toxic blooms, 73–76
aquatic life. *See also* algae; fish; food chains; invasive species; zooplankton
　environmental factors, 19, 46–47, 110, 128
　insects, 67, 108, 112, 114–15
　interconnectedness of species, 69, 70, 107–8, 110
　invertebrates, 35, 67, 73–77, 107, 110–11, 113, 131
　phantom midges, 47
　toxic contamination, 67–68, 89–90, 109, 124
　turtles, 119
aquatic plants
　ecosystem effects, 44, 59, 69–72, 74, 99, 107, 131
　environmental factors, 14, 65, 70
atmospheric moisture, 48–50, 53, 71

B
back shore, 63
bacteria, 35, 67, 73–76
beaches, 28, 62–64, 127
bio-concentration, 67–68, 89–90
biologic controls, 100, 133
biota. *See* aquatic life
birds, 80–88, 108, 113, 131–32
boats as vectors for exotics, 95, 113, 133
bottom-up effect, 92
botulism, avian, 108, 131
bryozoans, 113

Burlington Bay, 55–57

C
calcium, 8, 56, 65, 93, 119
canals, 11, 18, 97, 98, 103, 133
carbon dioxide, 8, 71, 76, 134–35
Carey, Richard Adams, 106
Carleton's Prize, 48–49
carp, 69, 91
catchments. *See* drainage basins
cedar bluffs, 64–66
Champlain, Samuel de, 14–15
Champlain Canal, 16, 18, 133
Champlain Sea, 5–6, 90–91
Champlain Valley, 4–9
changeover, 24–26
climate, 13–14, 53, 54, 134–35
Columnaris disease, 94
contradictions of Lake Champlain, 19
copepods, 110–11
Crown Point, 8, 82
Crown Point Bridge, 16, 17, 18
Cumberland Bay, 55, 124
currents, 26, 46–48, 63, 110. *See also* internal seiche; waves
cyanobacteria (blue-green algae), 73–76

D
dams, 40, 103, 106, 132
DDT, 81, 84
dead zone, 19
decaying plant matter, 44, 45, 66–68, 72
de Champlain, Samuel. *See* Champlain, Samuel de
degrees of separation, 107–8
deltas. *See* river deltas
depth
　effects, 14, 21, 27–30, 69–70, 71
　of Lake Champlain, 10, 12–13, 18, 25
development. *See* human-induced impacts
diatoms, 35, 76–77

die-offs, 94, 99, 108
diffuse aquatic interactions, 107–8
diseases, 93–95, 108, 131
dispersal of species, 64, 90, 112–13, 117, 132
dolomite, 8, 65
double-crested cormorants, 80–82, 132
drainage basins, 11–12, 14–16, 21, 24, 127
ducks, 85–88, 108, 113
Duerr, Adam, 80
dunes, 63–64

E
economic factors, 129–31, 133, 137–38
ecosystem effects, 13–14, 81, 107–8, 124, 135
ecosystem services, 137–38
eel, American, 103–4, 125
eelgrass, 133
Ellrott, Brian, 101, 102
endangered species, 92, 104–6
energy transfer
　factors affecting, 31, 35–36, 128
　food chains, 67, 68, 77
　heat, 13–14, 29, 34, 89
　water movement as, 27–28, 31, 33, 39, 40, 63
erosion
　human-induced, 39, 40, 41, 136
　natural forces, 8, 27, 28, 38, 63
　water quality effects, 12, 128
Eurasian water milfoil, 70, 71–72, 99, 131
evaporation, 26, 48, 136
exotics. *See* introduced species; invasive species

F
Facey, Doug, 91–92
farmer's markets, 130
farming. *See* agriculture
faults, 7–8, 13
fertilizers, 127, 139
fetch, 27, 53
fish. *See also* invasive species; *individual species*
　as algae management, 69–70

congregation at transition zones, 30
diseases, 93, 94–95
forage, 47, 93, 132
migration (dispersal), 90–91
Mysis shrimp introductions, 109–10
species diversity, 91–92
top predators, 90, 93
toxic contamination of flesh, 89–90, 109, 124
fisheries
　commercial, 103–4, 106
　control of nuisance species, 82, 98, 100, 133
　management, 80, 101–2, 109–10, 132
　sport, 69–70, 93, 109–10, 133
Flexibacter columnaris, 94
flood level, 25
floodwaters, 60, 68
flow pathways, 14–15
foam, 44–46
fog, 48–50
food chains. *See also* forage species
　algae blooms, 69–70, 74, 107, 136
　competition, 99–101, 110
　distribution, 47
　dynamics, 69–70, 77, 79, 88–90, 92–93, 107, 132, 136
　effect on terrestrial ecosystems, 108, 110
　invasive species, 99–100, 113, 131, 132
　muck feeders, 69, 105
　nutrient sources, 35, 66–70, 69–72, 76
　toxic contamination, 89–90, 109, 124
forage species. *See also* algae; food chains; zooplankton
　aquatic plants, 72, 133
　fish, 82, 98, 99, 100, 109, 132
　forage base, 59, 67, 92–93
　invertebrates, 47, 109–10, 122
formation of Lake Champlain, 4–9, 11–12, 90–91
freezing. *See also* ice

INDEX

factors affecting, 36, 135–36
freeze-over and water dynamics, 30, 100, 118, 136
ice formation, 35–38
lake ice local effects, 38, 54
overwintering and aquatic life, 100, 117, 122

G

gases, 44, 45. *See also* carbon dioxide; oxygen
gas seepage, 55, 57
General, the, 55–57
geography of Lake Champlain, 17–19
geologic factors, 6–9, 13, 14
geomorphic assessment, 40
glaciation effects, 4–6, 11
global warming, 134–35
grabens, 7–8
Grand Isle, 8, 18, 19
gravity, 14–15, 17, 31
Great Lakes, 10–12, 90, 97–98, 113, 133. *See also individual Great Lakes*
greenhouse warming. *See* global warming
groundwater upwelling, 55–57
gulls, 82–84, 108
Gut, the, 17, 31

H

heat, 13–14, 29, 34, 48, 88, 134
heavy metals. *See* pollutants
hibernation, 117–18
history, Lake Champlain in, 48–49
hitchhiking species, 113, 117
Hudson River, 133
human-induced impacts
algae blooms, 18–21, 69–70, 73–76, 136, 139
environmental changes, 12, 41, 64, 123, 125–31, 134–35
invasive species, 90–91, 95, 113, 133
mitigation, 45, 66, 124, 137, 139–40
unintended consequences, 40, 82, 107–8, 130
hydrologic connections, 11

I

ice, 30, 35–38. *See also* freezing
impervious surfaces, 123, 125, 126, 127, 128–29
in-flowing water, 24
Inland Sea, 18–19, 24, 32
insects, 67, 112, 114–15
interconnectedness of species, 107–8
Intergovernmental Panel on Climate Change, 134
internal mixing processes, 14, 20, 29–33, 122. *See also* stratification
internal seiche, 31–33, 56. *See also* currents; waves
intrinsic values, 137–38
introduced species, 90–91, 99, 109–10, 132. *See also* invasive species
invasive species. *See also* food chains; introduced species; zebra mussels
diseases, 94–95, 108, 131
dispersal, 18, 95, 113, 117, 133
effects, 101, 124, 131–33
fish, 96–101, 107, 108, 131
invertebrates, 107, 113, 131
plants, 70–72, 99, 131
Isle La Motte, 8

K

Kingsland Bay, 63, 66

L

lag times, 123–24
Lake Champlain basin, 11, 14–16, 19, 126
Lake Champlain Committee (LCC), 139
lake ecosystems
effects of aquatic life, 92–93, 131–33
interconnectedness of species, 69–70, 93, 107–8
as mirrors of the past, 121–24
Lake Erie, 10, 24, 100, 108, 131
Lake Huron, 30, 97, 102
lake influence, 13–14, 53, 54
lake levels. *See* water levels
lake management, 11, 12, 69–70, 91, 131
Lake Michigan, 30, 97, 102
Lake Ontario, 10, 14, 97, 108, 131
Lake Superior
aquatic life, 97, 100, 102
physical properties, 12, 14, 24, 30
Lake Vermont, 4–5, 11–12
land use impacts. *See* human-induced impacts
Langmuir circulation, 46–48
layering. *See* stratification
Leahy, Senator Patrick, 19
light. *See* sunlight
limestone, 8, 65

M

Main Lake, 17, 18, 24, 31, 33, 35, 136
Malletts Bay, 17, 18, 24, 31
Manley, Pat, 55
Manley, Tom, 33, 55
Marangelo, Paul, 117
Marsden, Ellen, 101, 102
migratory birds, 84, 85–88
Mihuc, Tim, 111
milfoil. *See* Eurasian water milfoil
mirages, 50–52
Mishe-Nahma, King of Fishes, 104–6
Missisquoi Bay, 12, 14, 19, 24, 74, 92–94
Missisquoi National Wildlife Refuge, 82
Missisquoi River, 15, 16, 17, 19, 60
mixing. *See* internal mixing processes
mussels, 116–17, 131

N

nonnative species. *See* introduced species; invasive species
Northeast Arm. *See* Inland Sea
northern pike, 92, 93, 94
nuisance species, 132, 133
nutrient pollution
effects, 67–68, 74, 92, 124, 139
mitigation, 18, 60, 68–70, 139–40
sources, 12, 20–21, 26, 66–68, 70, 125–29, 136
nutrients
storage, 21, 26, 69–70, 124
transfer, 35, 108, 109

O

opossum shrimp, 109–10, 122
overfishing, 96, 106, 125, 132
overwintering, 117–18, 122
oxygen
aquatic life, 118, 119
effects, 67–68, 124
levels, 19, 29, 44, 72
sources, 48, 67–68, 71

P

particulate suspension. *See* suspended particles
passive feeding, 100
pavement. *See* impervious surfaces
PCBs, 89–90, 109, 124
Pearce, Fred, 134
periodic events, 122–24
Philosopher Fish, The, 106
phosphorus, 26, 70, 74, 125–29, 136, 139
Pientka, Bernie, 92
plankton. *See* zooplankton
plant cover, 21, 26, 63–68, 128, 134
plants, water. *See* aquatic plants
pockmarks, 55–57
politics and environment, 124
pollutants. *See also* nutrient pollution
accumulation, 26, 109, 124, 128
effect on biota, 82, 84, 89–90, 109
heavy metals, 89–90, 128
mercury, 89–90, 109, 124
pesticides, 81, 84
sources, 45, 125–29
toxic chemicals, 26, 109, 124, 139
Potash Brook, 125–26
precipitation, 25, 26, 136
predator-prey dynamics. *See* food chains
predictability, 122–24, 125, 135–36
protection of Lake Champlain

efforts needed, 45, 66, 124, 137, 139–40
public perceptions, 11, 12, 75, 131

Q
quasi-liquid, 36–37

R
rainbow smelt, 82, 100, 109, 132
rainwater. *See also* stormwater runoff
absorption and retention, 17, 25, 26, 126, 128
acidic nature, 8
flow pathways, 14–16
recreational use
impacts on, 75–76, 95, 113, 127, 131, 133
sport fishing, 69–70, 93, 109–10
value, 137, 138
Red Rock Point, 18
retention time, 24–26
Richelieu River, 14–15, 18, 25, 63, 103
Riley, Jake, 102
river deltas, 9, 18, 60–62
rivers, 14–15, 35, 39–41, 61–63, 66–68
roads. *See* impervious surfaces
round goby, 107, 108, 131
runoff. *See* stormwater runoff

S
salmon, 96, 109–10, 125, 132, 136
sand, 62–64
Schmitz, Sonja, 64
sea lamprey, viii–ix, 93, 96–98, 132
seasonal changes, 25, 29–30, 31, 33–34, 52–54, 122
sedimentation, 9, 19, 39, 60–63, 128
sediments
aquatic life and, 69, 77, 105, 107
nutrients and pollutants, 21, 26, 70, 109, 124, 128
sources and movement, 30, 38–39, 68, 125–29
sewage treatment, 70
shallow water, 14, 29, 32, 69–70
shorelines, 27, 28, 38, 60–66
size, 10, 12–14, 27, 36, 53–54, 88
sloshing. *See* internal seiche
small-world hypothesis, 107
snow, 36, 52–54
soil, 44, 126
Song of Hiawatha, 104–6
Sorenson, Eric, 65–66
South Burlington, Vermont, 125
South Lake, 16, 17–18, 24
species migration. *See* dispersal of species
sport fisheries. *See* fisheries
St. Albans Bay, 19, 20, 70
St. Lawrence River, 11
St-Jean-sur-Richelieu, 14, 17
storms, 52–54, 122–23, 136
stormwater runoff
effect, 12, 39, 77, 123–25, 136
impaired waterways, 41, 125–29
management, 128
stratification, 14, 29, 30, 135–36. *See also* internal mixing processes
streaking, 46–48
streams, 26, 41, 125–29
sturgeon, 104–6, 125
sunlight, 20, 33–35, 51, 68, 71, 77, 88
surface active (surfactants), 44
surface area, 10, 12–14, 14, 21, 27
surface seiche, 31
surface tension, 44, 114
suspended particles, 35, 44
Suter, Robert, 114

T
temperature. *See* air temperature; water temperature
Tendy, Bob, 52
thermoclines, 29, 31–33, 46
thiaminase, 99
Thompson, Elizabeth, 65–66
Thompson, Zadock, 105
Thompson's Point, 18, 87
topography effects, 20–21, 39, 40, 49, 68
toxic chemicals. *See* pollutants
trees. *See* plant cover
tributaries of Lake Champlain, 18, 19
trout, 90–91, 94, 96–97, 99, 101–2, 109–10, 125, 132, 136
turnover. *See* internal mixing processes
turtles, 118–19

U
underwater waves. *See* internal seiche
unintended consequences. *See* human-induced impacts
upwelling currents, 46

V
Valcour Island, 48, 66
value of Lake Champlain, viii–ix, 137–38
vertical migration, 47, 109–10, 122
volume, lake, 12, 13–14, 25–26, 35–36

W
wastewater treatment, 21
water. *See also* freezing; internal mixing processes
chemistry, 26, 56, 74
gases in solution, 8, 44, 45, 71, 76, 134–35
molecular behavior, 27, 29–31, 36–38, 44, 114, 115
physical properties, 29–30, 31–32, 36, 44–46, 114
water chestnut, 18, 99, 131
water clarity
aquatic life effects, 18, 70, 99, 100, 107
effects, 35, 44, 69, 70
water column dynamics, 47, 56
water column migration. *See* vertical migration
water levels, 25, 55, 136
water plants. *See* aquatic plants
water quality. *See* algae; nutrient pollution; pollutants; stormwater runoff
watershed, 11
water temperature
air-water differential, 48, 51–52
determinants, 13–14, 31, 33–34
effects, 20, 29, 30, 44, 46, 68, 136
thermoclines, 29, 31–33, 33
waterways, commercial. *See* canals
waves, 27–28, 32–33, 44, 63. *See also* currents; internal seiche
Weart, Spencer, 134
weather. *See also* stormwater runoff
effects, 29, 30, 94, 100, 122–23
patterns, 13, 52–54, 125, 136
weeds. *See* aquatic plants
Watzin, Mary, 56
wildlife management, 82, 91, 95
Willsboro Bay, 19, 20, 21
wind
aquatic life, 20, 113, 115
lake influence, 13, 53–54
surface effects, 36, 44, 46, 63
water movement, 14, 27, 29, 31
Winooski River, 9, 11, 16, 18, 90
winter, 30, 117–18, 122. *See also* freezing
Wright, Steven, 5–6

Z
zebra mussels
dispersal, 18, 56, 93, 113, 124
economic impacts, 131
native species impacts, 18, 74, 93, 111–12, 117, 125, 131
and other exotics, 101, 107
water quality, 18, 70, 99, 107
zooplankton
distribution, 46–47
predator-prey dynamics, 69–70, 77, 92–93, 99, 100, 107
species diversity, 110–12, 113, 131